The Anti-Inflammatory Diet for Beginners

A Stress-Free Handbook with Budget-Friendly Meals to Boost Wellness, Decrease Inflammation & Achieve Lasting Health + Bonus Natural Anti-Inflammatory Guide

Dr. Madison Wells

Table Of Content:

Chapter 6:
Nourishing Mains: Fish, Poultry & Vegetarian

Introduction

The Power of Food to Fight Inflammation: Your Roadmap to Optimal Health

In the lush landscape of health and wellness, there stands a potent, yet often overlooked hero: food. This isn't about the latest fad diet or a restrictive list of do's and don'ts. It's about understanding how certain foods can act as powerful allies in your battle against chronic inflammation, guiding you towards a state of wellbeing you may have thought was out of reach. This chapter opens the door to a fresh perspective on the anti-inflammatory diet, aiming not just to inform but to empower you on your journey to optimal health.

Understanding the Impact of Chronic Inflammation

Before diving into the transformative power of food, it's crucial to grasp the significance of chronic inflammation and its pervasive effects on our health. Unlike acute inflammation—a necessary process that helps your body heal from injuries—chronic inflammation is a low-grade, persistent state that can stealthily undermine your health, laying the groundwork for a myriad of diseases.

From heart disease to rheumatoid arthritis, from diabetes to Alzheimer's, the shadow of chronic inflammation looms large. Yet, amidst this seemingly grim picture emerges a glimmer of hope. How you choose to fuel your body can turn the tides against this insidious foe.

Food: The Ultimate Weapon Against Inflammation

Imagine your kitchen as a pharmacy, each ingredient a remedy waiting to unleash its healing power. The anti-inflammatory diet isn't a one-size-fits-all prescription but a personalized approach to eating that emphasizes whole, nutrient-dense foods known to quell inflammation.

The Foundation of an Anti-Inflammatory Diet

Fruits and vegetables, rich in antioxidants, serve as the cornerstone of an anti-inflammatory diet. These vibrant foods counteract the oxidative stress that fuels inflammation, acting as a protective shield for your body. Whole grains, lean protein, and healthy fats from sources like fish, nuts, and avocados complement this foundation, offering a symphony of nutrients that work in harmony to reduce inflammation.

Herbs and spices, often relegated to the sidelines, deserve a spotlight for their potent anti-inflammatory effects. Turmeric, with its active compound curcumin, has garnered acclaim for its powerful anti-inflammatory and antioxidant properties. Ginger, cinnamon, and garlic are not far behind, each bringing their unique benefits to the table.

The Personal Touch

Adopting an anti-inflammatory diet is more than merely following a list of recommended foods; it's about tuning into your body's unique responses. Food sensitivities, which can vary widely from person to person, play a crucial role in managing inflammation. For some, dairy or gluten may exacerbate inflammation, necessitating a tailored approach to dietary choices.

This personalized strategy extends to meal planning and preparation. Simplicity is key. An anti-inflammatory diet doesn't require elaborate recipes or obscure ingredients; it's grounded in simplicity and sustainability. Quick, nourishing meals that align with your dietary needs and preferences make it easier to embrace this lifestyle long term.

Real-Life Transformations

The proof, as they say, is in the pudding—or in this case, in the vibrant, antioxidant-rich berries and leafy greens. Take Sarah, a 45-year-old teacher battling persistent joint pain and fatigue. After adopting an anti-inflammatory diet, focusing on whole foods and eliminating her personal triggers, she noticed a profound shift. Her pain diminished, her energy levels soared, and she reclaimed a sense of vitality she thought was lost.

Or consider Mark, a 50-year-old with a family history of heart disease. By incorporating more omega-3-rich foods like salmon and flaxseeds into his diet, he not only improved his lipid profile but also experienced an unexpected benefit: better mood and mental clarity.

In Closing: A Journey to Remember

Embracing the power of food to fight inflammation is a journey worth taking. It's a path paved with the promise of improved health, vitality, and well-being. As you embark on this journey, remember, this isn't about perfection or a quick fix. It's about making informed, mindful choices that nourish your body and soul, leading you to a state of health where you can thrive, not just survive.

Special Bonus

Before we embark on this transformative journey together, I am excited to share an exclusive gift that will significantly enhance your understanding and application of the anti-inflammatory principles we'll explore. "Surprising Anti-Inflammatory Benefits of Essential Oils & Natural Supplements" is not just an addendum to this book — it's a pivotal companion piece that sheds light on the subtle yet powerful influencers of inflammation. This bonus material delves into the nuanced world of natural therapeutics, elucidating how essential oils and supplements can synergistically enhance the dietary adjustments you will learn about.

What makes this bonus so indispensable is its focus on holistic healing. While diet lays the groundwork for managing inflammation, the addition of essential oils and natural supplements can fortify and accelerate your progress, offering a multifaceted approach to wellness. By incorporating this knowledge, you fully equip yourself with a comprehensive toolkit for anti-inflammatory living.

To access this exclusive content, simply scan the QR code provided within this book. With a quick scan, you'll be able to download your free copy of this indispensable resource.

Chapter 1:

Understanding Chronic Inflammation

1.1 What is Chronic Inflammation?

Chronic inflammation stands as a critical concept in understanding the body's response to various internal and external stressors. Unlike its acute counterpart—a short-term, protective reaction involving redness, swelling, and pain signaling the body's healing process—chronic inflammation is a more clandestine and persistent condition that may not manifest noticeable symptoms initially but can significantly impact health over time.

The Hidden Flame Within: Understanding Chronic Inflammation
At its core, chronic inflammation is an extended, often imperceptible immune response, where the body continuously deploys white blood cells and inflammatory markers to a perceived threat, even when such a threat is minimal or nonexistent. This prolonged state of alert can lead to an imbalance, affecting tissues, cells, and organs, thereby setting the stage for a myriad of chronic conditions and diseases.

Triggers and Troublemakers: The Causes of Chronic Inflammation
Several factors contribute to the development and sustenance of chronic inflammation. These include, but are not limited to, persistent infections, environmental pollutants, stress, sedentary lifestyle, and notably, dietary choices. Processed foods, high sugar intake, and excessive consumption of unhealthy fats can exacerbate the body's

inflammatory response, turning what is meant to be a protective mechanism into a potentially harmful, ongoing condition.

The Silent Saboteur: Consequences of Unchecked Inflammation

Chronic inflammation is insidious, often advancing unnoticed until significant damage occurs. This relentless inflammation can lay the groundwork for several diseases, such as cardiovascular disorders, diabetes, arthritis, and certain cancers, by damaging cells and tissues, altering genetic expression, and disrupting normal bodily functions.

The Dietary Defense: Combatting Inflammation Through Nutrition

Herein lies a silver lining—the profound impact of dietary choices on modulating the body's inflammatory processes. Integral to this book's ethos is the concept that specific foods and dietary patterns can effectively combat chronic inflammation. Emphasizing whole, nutrient-dense foods, rich in antioxidants, phytonutrients, healthy fats, and fibers, forms the cornerstone of an anti-inflammatory diet. This approach is not about stringent restrictions but about enriching one's diet with foods that nourish and protect the body, fostering a conducive environment for healing and optimal health.

Practical Pathways: A Forward-Thinking Approach

Embracing an anti-inflammatory diet does not necessitate a radical overhaul of one's lifestyle or culinary preferences. It is about making informed, pragmatic choices—selecting olive oil over refined vegetable oils, opting for colorful fruits and vegetables, incorporating lean proteins and whole grains, and reducing the intake of processed foods and sugars. Such changes, though seemingly small, can profoundly influence the body's inflammatory status and overall health trajectory.

In forging ahead, it is crucial to underscore the significance of awareness, education, and the application of knowledge regarding chronic inflammation and dietary management. Empowering individuals with the understanding and tools to make healthful dietary choices facilitates a proactive stance against chronic inflammation, encouraging a shift towards sustainable health and wellness practices.

As we delve deeper into the subsequent sections, we will explore the concrete elements of an anti-inflammatory diet, practical strategies for implementation, and supportive lifestyle adjustments. The aim is to provide a comprehensive, accessible guide that resonates with the concerns, aspirations, and realities of our intended audience, guiding them towards achieving and maintaining optimal health through dietary excellence and informed lifestyle choices.

1.2 The Toll of Unchecked Inflammation

The unchecked progression of chronic inflammation is akin to a silent alarm that never gets turned off, quietly undermining health without the obvious signs one might expect from an immediate threat. This persistent state of alert can gradually erode the body's defenses and integrity, leading to a wide array of health disorders that can severely impede quality of life. The toll of such inflammation is extensive, affecting numerous bodily systems and functions, manifesting in various diseases and conditions that are increasingly prevalent in today's society.

The Creeping Threat: How Chronic Inflammation Harms
Chronic inflammation's impact on health cannot be overstated. Over time, this smoldering fire within can contribute to the development of heart disease by promoting the build-up of plaque in the arteries, a condition known as atherosclerosis. It can incite insulin resistance, a precursor to type 2 diabetes, and interfere with fat metabolism, leading to obesity and complicating weight management efforts. The bones and joints are not spared, as chronic inflammation is a key player in the pathogenesis of osteoporosis and rheumatoid arthritis, respectively, undermining mobility and the joy of active living.

Moreover, chronic inflammation has been linked to neurodegenerative diseases such as Alzheimer's and Parkinson's, suggesting an intricate connection between systemic inflammation and brain health. It is implicated in the exacerbation of asthma and chronic obstructive pulmonary disease (COPD), making every breath a challenge for those affected. On a cellular level, sustained inflammation can foster an environment conducive to the initiation and progression of various cancers by inducing DNA damage and hampering the body's ability to repair genetic defects.

The Unseen Costs: Quality of Life and Economic Burden

The reach of chronic inflammation extends beyond physical health, deeply affecting emotional well-being and quality of life. The constant discomfort, pain, and the ensuing stress and anxiety can diminish an individual's capacity for joy, social interaction, and productivity. This erosion of quality of life is not just a personal tragedy but also carries a significant economic burden, with increased healthcare costs, lost productivity, and the profound impact on caregivers and families.

Nutrition and Lifestyle: A Beacon of Hope

While the challenges presented by chronic inflammation are daunting, there is potent hope in the power of modifiable lifestyle factors, particularly nutrition. An anti-inflammatory diet, rich in fruits, vegetables, whole grains, lean protein, and healthy fats, can significantly reduce the levels of inflammatory markers in the body. Simple dietary shifts, such as increasing the intake of omega-3 fatty acids found in fatty fish and flaxseed, can have profound anti-inflammatory effects. Similarly, reducing the consumption of processed foods, sugary drinks, and trans fats can dampen the fires of inflammation.

Equally important is the role of regular physical activity, adequate sleep, stress management, and avoidance of known inflammatory triggers like smoking and excessive alcohol consumption. These lifestyle choices can fortify the body's defenses against the silent assault of chronic inflammation, mitigating its toll on the body and enhancing overall well-being.

1.3 The Gut-Immune System Connection

The connection between the gut and the immune system emerges as a profound partnership, pivotal to our health and well-being. Dubbed the gut-immune system connection, this relationship holds the key to understanding not just chronic inflammation, but also the path towards mitigating its effects through mindful nutrition and lifestyle choices.

The Gut: A Fortress of Immunity

The human gut is more than a digestive organ; it's a bustling metropolis of microorganisms, a vast ecosystem that plays a critical role in our immune response. In this complex milieu, beneficial bacteria work tirelessly to digest food, synthesize essential vitamins, and form a defensive barrier against harmful pathogens. Remarkably, the gut houses approximately 70% of our immune cells, making it a central command post for detecting and responding to microbial threats.

The Immune Response: A Delicate Balance

When the gut's delicate balance is disrupted, the immune system takes note, often responding with inflammation to combat perceived threats. This mechanism is vital for healing and protection under normal circumstances. However, when inflammation becomes chronic, it can inadvertently damage the body's own tissues, leading to a cascade of health issues.

Dysbiosis: When the Balance Tips

Dysbiosis, an imbalance in the gut microbiota, can trigger this unwelcome inflammatory response. Factors such as poor diet, stress, antibiotic overuse, and environmental toxins contribute to this imbalance, compromising the intestinal barrier and allowing endotoxins to enter the bloodstream. This phenomenon, known as "leaky gut," signals the immune system to launch a defense, igniting an inflammatory response that, if unchecked, becomes a perpetual cycle of discomfort and disease.

The Connection to Chronic Diseases

The implications of a compromised gut-immune system connection are vast. Research indicates a direct link between gut health and a variety of chronic diseases, including autoimmune disorders like rheumatoid arthritis and inflammatory bowel disease, as well as metabolic syndrome, type 2 diabetes, and even certain cancers. These conditions underscore the critical nature of maintaining gut health for overall immune system function and inflammation control.

Nourishing the Gut-Immune Alliance

The power of food to either harm or heal this connection cannot be underestimated. A diet rich in processed, high-sugar, and high-fat foods can exacerbate dysbiosis and inflammation, while a diverse, nutrient-dense diet supports a healthy gut microbiome and strengthens the immune response. Foods high in fiber, such as fruits, vegetables, and whole grains, serve as fuel for beneficial gut bacteria, promoting their growth and activity. Fermented foods like yogurt, kefir, and sauerkraut introduce beneficial probiotics, aiding in the restoration of the gut's microbial balance.

1.4 How an Anti-Inflammatory Diet Can Help

Embracing the Anti-Inflammatory Diet: A Pathway to Wellness

At the core of managing and mitigating chronic inflammation lies a powerful, yet often underestimated ally: your diet. The shift toward an anti-inflammatory diet is not merely about subtracting certain foods from your plate; it's about filling your life with meals that heal, nourish, and revitalize your body from the inside out. This transition can significantly dial down inflammation, thus enhancing your health and vitality, and steering you away from the discomfort and risks associated with chronic inflammation.

The Scientific Backdrop

Extensive research underscores the link between diet and inflammation. Foods high in refined sugars, trans fats, and processed ingredients can exacerbate inflammatory responses, potentially leading to a state of chronic inflammation. Conversely, a meticulously curated anti-inflammatory diet, abundant in whole, nutrient-rich foods, can act as a buffer against inflammation, mending the body's intricate systems in a myriad of ways.

The Foundation of an Anti-Inflammatory Diet

At its heart, an anti-inflammatory diet promotes a return to the basics — a diet emphasizing whole foods that our ancestors would recognize. The pillars of such a diet include fruits, vegetables, lean proteins, whole grains, and healthy fats, all chosen for their ability to reduce inflammation and support overall health. Such foods are packed with antioxidants, phytonutrients, vitamins, and minerals that serve as the body's natural defense against oxidative stress, a key contributor to inflammation.

The Power of Phytonutrients

Phytonutrients, found in a rainbow of fruits and vegetables, are compounds that have been shown to have significant anti-inflammatory properties. These substances go beyond essential nutrients to fight inflammation at its root, bolstering the immune system and protecting against chronic diseases. Integrating a spectrum of colorful produce into your diet ensures a broad array of these protective compounds.

Omega-3 Fatty Acids: The Anti-Inflammatory Heavyweights

Healthy fats, particularly omega-3 fatty acids found in fish like salmon and plant sources like flaxseeds, wield considerable power in quelling inflammation. These fats are essential for the body's well-being, supporting heart health, brain function, and reducing inflammation levels. Incorporating these fats into your diet can help shift the balance from pro-inflammatory foods to a more healthful, anti-inflammatory nutritional profile.

The Role of Fiber in Gut Health and Inflammation

Fiber, abundant in whole grains, fruits, and vegetables, acts as a prebiotic, nourishing beneficial gut bacteria and facilitating a healthy gut microbiome. A robust gut is fundamental in mitigating inflammation, as it prevents the release of pro-inflammatory substances into the bloodstream. Thus, a diet rich in fiber can significantly impact inflammation and overall health.

Simplifying the Anti-Inflammatory Diet for Everyday Living

Adopting an anti-inflammatory diet may seem daunting, especially within a society where processed foods are ubiquitous and time is scarce. However, simplifying this approach can make it both attainable and sustainable:

- Focus on adding color to your plate with a variety of fruits and vegetables.
- Choose whole grains over refined ones to maximize nutritional intake and minimize inflammatory responses.
- Opt for lean sources of protein, such as poultry, fish, beans, and legumes, to support muscle health and reduce fat intake.
- Integrate healthy fats from avocados, nuts, seeds, and olive oil to combat inflammation.
- Hydrate with water, herbal teas, and other low-sugar beverages to support detoxification and hydration, essential for reducing inflammation.

The Journey Forward

Embracing an anti-inflammatory diet is not about stringent restrictions or overwhelming changes. It's about making deliberate, healthful choices that nourish and sustain your body, creating a diet that works for you, not against you. By focusing on nutrient-rich, anti-inflammatory foods, you can effectively reduce inflammation, enhance your well-being, and embark on a path toward a healthier, more vibrant life.

With each meal, you have the opportunity to influence your health positively. Let the principles of the anti-inflammatory diet guide you towards making choices that foster wellness, vitality, and longevity, turning the tide against chronic inflammation and opening the door to a life filled with energy and vitality.

Chapter 2:

Getting Started on the Anti-Inflammatory Diet

2.1 Determining Your Dietary Needs

Embarking on an anti-inflammatory diet begins with a deeply personal step: understanding and determining your unique dietary needs. This is a crucial starting point that paves the way for nutritional choices aligning with your body's specific requirements and health goals.

The Individuality of Dietary Needs

No two individuals are identical, and similarly, no single diet fits all. The intricacy of our biological makeup means that each person's response to certain foods can vastly differ. Some might thrive on a diet heavy in grains and legumes, while others might find these cause discomfort or inflammation. Recognizing and respecting this individual variability is essential in crafting a diet that supports rather than undermines your health.

The Role of Personal Health History

Your journey begins with a reflective look at your personal health history. This includes understanding any chronic conditions, food sensitivities, allergies, and other health concerns that might dictate specific dietary needs. Common conditions such as diabetes, cardiovascular disease, and autoimmune disorders require a nuanced approach to diet, emphasizing foods that aid in managing these conditions while avoiding those that could exacerbate symptoms.

Getting Proficient with Nutritional Labels

A fundamental skill in determining your dietary needs is becoming proficient in reading and understanding nutritional labels. This involves more than just scanning for calorie counts; it's about identifying ingredient lists for hidden sources of sugars, processed fats, and additives that could ignite inflammatory responses. Educating yourself on these elements helps navigate the complexities of food choices, steering you toward options that support your anti-inflammatory goals.

Integrating Variety: The Spice of Life and Health

Once you've established the dietary no-go zones based on your health history and sensitivities, the next step is to ensure variety within the parameters of an anti-inflammatory diet. Incorporating a broad spectrum of foods not only prevents nutritional deficiencies but also shields your body from potential adverse effects of over-consuming any single food group. This diverse approach allows you to explore a wide array of nutrients—each playing a unique role in combatting inflammation and bolstering your health.

Listening to Your Body: The Ultimate Guide

Despite all the scientific guidance and expert advice, one of your most valuable tools in determining dietary needs is your body's feedback. Listening attentively to your body—observing how it reacts to specific foods or dietary patterns—provides real-time, personalized insights that no generic diet plan can offer. This involves tuning into signals such as energy levels, digestive comfort, skin health, and overall well-being post-meal consumption.

Embracing Flexibility and Patience

Adopting an anti-inflammatory diet tailored to your needs is not an overnight process. It requires patience, flexibility, and the willingness to adapt as your body and health status evolve. Dietary needs can change in response to age, lifestyle modifications, and health changes, necessitating periodic reassessment and possibly recalibration of your nutritional approach.

Collaborate with Professionals for Tailored Advice

While embarking on this journey independently is possible, seeking the expertise of health professionals—such as dietitians, nutritionists, or functional medicine doctors—can provide tailored guidance. These experts can help interpret your body's signals, understand your health history, and design a personalized dietary plan that enhances your anti-inflammatory quest.

2.2 Identifying Food Sensitivities

Food sensitivities differ significantly from food allergies. While allergies trigger immediate and potentially life-threatening reactions, sensitivities may cause milder yet chronic symptoms, making them harder to pinpoint. These can range from digestive upset, skin rashes, headaches, fatigue, to joint pain—symptoms often associated with chronic inflammation. Recognizing these sensitivities allows you to tailor your diet to mitigate such adverse reactions.

The Interplay Between Diet and Inflammation

The foods we eat can profoundly affect inflammation in our bodies. Certain dietary components, like processed sugars and trans fats, are notorious for their pro-inflammatory effects. Conversely, whole foods rich in omega-3 fatty acids, antioxidants, and phytonutrients can significantly dampen inflammatory responses. Understanding your food sensitivities enables you to make informed decisions, pivoting towards choices that support your inflammation-fighting objectives.

Strategies to Uncover Food Sensitivities

One effective approach to identifying your sensitivities is the elimination diet. This involves removing common culprits, such as gluten, dairy, soy, and refined sugars, from your diet for a set period, typically three to four weeks. Following this phase, you'll gradually reintroduce these foods one at a time, observing your body's reactions. This method requires patience and diligence but can be incredibly revealing, shedding light on how specific foods impact your health and well-being.

Listening to Your Body: A Personal Detective Story

As you navigate the process of identifying food sensitivities, becoming attuned to your body's signals is paramount. This means paying attention to subtle cues and symptoms that may arise following the consumption of certain foods. Do you feel unusually tired after eating grains? Does your skin flare up after dairy intake? These observations are vital clues in your detective work to uncover the dietary sources of discomfort and inflammation.

The Role of Food Journals in Identifying Triggers

Keeping a detailed food journal is a practical and effective tool in this investigative process. Document not just what you eat, but also how you feel physically and emotionally afterward. Over time, patterns can emerge, offering invaluable insights into foods that may not agree with you. This evidence-based approach makes it easier to make adjustments and personalized dietary choices that enhance your health.

2.3 The Elimination Diet Approach

The elimination diet approach is a powerful tool in this journey, designed to identify food sensitivities that might be contributing to inflammation and overall discomfort. This section will guide you through the implementation of an elimination diet, outlining strategic steps to uncover how your body reacts to different foods and how you can adapt your diet to support your health and well-being.

The Foundation of the Elimination Diet

The elimination diet is grounded in the principle of removing potential food triggers from your diet for a period, then systematically reintroducing them to observe any changes in symptoms. This approach is not a one-size-fits-all solution; rather, it's a personalized expedition to discover your unique dietary sensitivities and their impact on inflammation and health.

Starting Your Journey

The first step is to identify the common inflammatory food culprits, including gluten, dairy, soy, corn, eggs, and processed sugars. These are removed from your diet for a period—usually three to six weeks—which serves as a reset for your system, allowing inflammation to subside and providing a clean baseline from which to identify sensitivities.

During this phase, the focus is on consuming whole, unprocessed foods that are known for their anti-inflammatory properties. Think colorful fruits and vegetables, lean proteins, healthy fats, and whole grains (excluding those you're eliminating, such as wheat, if gluten is a suspected sensitivity). This is not merely about restriction but about nourishing your body with foods that promote healing and well-being.

Listening to Your Body

The most critical aspect of the elimination diet is attentiveness to your body's responses. During the elimination phase, take note of any changes in symptoms you may have been experiencing, such as digestive discomfort, fatigue, skin issues, or joint pain. An improvement in these symptoms can indicate that one or more of the eliminated foods may be a trigger for you.

The Reintroduction Phase

After the elimination period, you will slowly reintroduce the removed foods one at a time, carefully observing any symptomatic changes. Each food should be reintroduced over a few days, allowing sufficient time to monitor potential reactions before moving on to the next. This painstaking process is crucial for accurately pinpointing which foods your body can tolerate and which provoke inflammatory responses.

It's essential to approach this phase with patience and an open mind. The goal is not to restrict your diet indefinitely but to gain insights that will allow you to make the most healthful choices for your body.

Documenting Your Findings

Keeping a detailed food and symptom journal is invaluable throughout this process. Record not only what you eat and when but also any physical or emotional reactions. This journal becomes an indispensable tool for identifying patterns that connect specific foods with symptoms, guiding your dietary choices moving forward.

2.4 Anti-Inflammatory Diet Fundamentals

Embarking on an anti-inflammatory diet represents a pivotal choice towards embracing a lifestyle dedicated to fostering health and combating inflammation. This choice, while highly effective, brings forth concerns about complexity, affordability, and long-term sustainability. However, the core principle of this diet is simplicity—focusing on whole, nutrient-dense foods that naturally lower inflammation levels in the body. This section delves into the fundamentals of an anti-inflammatory diet, providing you with a solid foundation to make this dietary approach an enjoyable and sustainable part of your life.

Embrace Whole Foods

At the heart of an anti-inflammatory diet lies the commitment to whole, unprocessed foods. These foods are the building blocks of a healthful eating plan, rich in vitamins, minerals, fiber, and antioxidants, which support the body's natural ability to fight inflammation. Incorporating a diverse array of colorful vegetables and fruits, whole grains, lean proteins, and healthy fats ensures a broad spectrum of nutrients essential for reducing inflammation and promoting overall well-being.

Prioritize Anti-Inflammatory Powerhouses

Certain foods are renowned for their anti-inflammatory properties, serving as powerful allies in your health journey. These include:

- **Omega-3-rich foods:** Cold-water fish like salmon, mackerel, and sardines, along with flaxseeds and walnuts, are excellent sources of omega-3 fatty acids, known for their potent anti-inflammatory effects.
- **Antioxidant-packed fruits and vegetables:** Berries, leafy greens, and other brightly colored fruits and vegetables are high in antioxidants, which help neutralize free radicals, reducing inflammation and protecting against disease.
- **Healthful fats:** Olive oil, avocados, and nuts are rich in monounsaturated fats and polyphenols, promoting heart health and supporting anti-inflammatory processes.

- **Spices and herbs:** Turmeric, ginger, garlic, and cinnamon are just a few examples of spices and herbs that have been celebrated for their anti-inflammatory and health-promoting properties.

Moderate Inflammatory Foods

While focusing on anti-inflammatory foods, it's equally vital to limit or avoid those that can trigger or exacerbate inflammation. Processed and refined foods, high in sugar and unhealthy fats, are primary culprits, along with excessive alcohol and processed meats. By minimizing these in your diet, you're taking solid steps toward diminishing chronic inflammation and enhancing your health.

Consistency Over Perfection

Adopting an anti-inflammatory diet is not about adhering to a strict regimen or achieving perfection. Instead, it's about making consistent, healthful choices that support your body's well-being. This approach allows for flexibility and the occasional indulgence, ensuring that the diet remains practical, enjoyable, and sustainable in the long term.

The Role of Hydration

Hydration is a cornerstone of health, playing a critical role in every cellular process in our bodies, including the management of inflammation. Drinking ample water throughout the day helps flush toxins from the body, supports digestion, and ensures that your cells are functioning optimally.

Making It Affordable

A common concern is the perceived high cost of an anti-inflammatory diet. However, focusing on whole foods rather than specialized "health foods" can make this eating plan more budget-friendly. Seasonal produce, bulk grains and legumes, and choosing frozen over fresh options for certain items are all strategies to enjoy the benefits of an anti-inflammatory diet without overspending. Planning meals in advance and cooking at home can also significantly reduce costs while giving you complete control over the ingredients you use.

Chapter 3:

Anti-Inflammatory Pantry Essentials

3.1 Key Nutrients that Reduce Inflammation

Understanding the pivotal role of certain nutrients in quelling inflammation lays the groundwork for a diet that not only nourishes but heals. These nutrients work synergistically within your body, akin to a finely tuned orchestra, each playing a critical role in diminishing inflammatory processes and promoting overall health.

- **Omega-3 Fatty Acids: The Inflammation-Busting Heroes**

Omega-3 fatty acids are renowned for their potent anti-inflammatory properties. Found abundantly in fatty fish like salmon, mackerel, and sardines, as well as flaxseeds and chia seeds, omega-3s work by reducing the production of molecules and substances linked to inflammation, such as eicosanoids and cytokines.

Incorporating omega-3-rich foods into your diet doesn't have to be a daunting task. Simple swaps, like choosing salmon over red meat a few times a week or adding a sprinkle of ground flaxseeds to your morning oatmeal, can make a significant impact on your inflammation levels.

- **Antioxidants: Nature's Inflammation Fighters**

Antioxidants play a crucial role in neutralizing free radicals, harmful molecules that can cause cell damage and inflammation. Vitamins C and E, selenium, and carotenoids are just a few examples of antioxidants that can help protect your body against inflammation.

The spectrum of antioxidant-rich foods is vast, including berries, nuts, dark leafy greens, and whole grains. By ensuring a colorful plate at each meal, you're not only making your meal visually appealing but are also providing your body with an array of antioxidants essential for fighting inflammation.

- **Fiber: The Gut Health Guardian**

Fiber is a crucial nutrient for maintaining a healthy gut, an important aspect of preventing and reducing inflammation. Beyond its well-known benefits for digestion, fiber helps to nourish beneficial gut bacteria, which play a role in reducing inflammation.

Whole grains, legumes, vegetables, and fruits are excellent sources of fiber. Incorporate these into your meals in creative ways, such as adding beans to salads, snacking on fruit, or opting for whole-grain versions of your favorite breads and pastas.

- **Polyphenols: Tiny but Mighty Inflammation Warriors**

Polyphenols are micronutrients packed with antioxidants, found in a wide variety of plants. They've gained attention for their ability to reduce inflammation and even lower the risk of certain diseases.

Foods rich in polyphenols include berries, green tea, dark chocolate, and even some spices like turmeric. Integrating these into your diet can be as delightful as savoring a cup of green tea in the afternoon or indulging in a square of dark chocolate as a treat.

- **Streamlining Anti-Inflammatory Nutrients into Your Diet**

The key to a sustainable anti-inflammatory diet lies not in a complete overhaul of your pantry and eating habits overnight but in making mindful, gradual additions and substitutions. Start by introducing one or two anti-inflammatory foods into each meal.

Experiment with cooking methods and recipes that highlight these ingredients' natural flavors and nutritional benefits.

Remember, your diet should be a reflection of balance and variety, providing a holistic approach to fighting inflammation. Each nutrient plays a unique role in this process, and together, they can help steer you toward a healthier, more vibrant life.

3.2 Stocking Up on Healthy Fats

The term 'fat' has often been stigmatized, leading many to erroneously eschew it from their diets. However, not all fats are created equal, and distinguishing between those that fuel inflammation and those that fight it is key to transforming your health. In this section, we delve into how integrating healthy fats into your pantry can create a foundation for long-lasting wellness, particularly for those navigating the realm of anti-inflammatory eating.

Embracing the Good: The Role of Healthy Fats

Healthy fats constitute a cornerstone of anti-inflammatory nutrition. These fats are instrumental not just in reducing inflammation but in numerous vital functions such as hormone production, cell membrane integrity, and nutrient absorption. Moreover, they are essential for brain health and maintaining energy levels. By incorporating sources of these nutritious fats into your diet, you're not just combating inflammation but nurturing your body holistically.

Monounsaturated fats and polyunsaturated fats, including omega-3 fatty acids, stand out for their anti-inflammatory properties.

Monounsaturated fats, found in foods such as avocados, olive oil, and nuts, are celebrated for their ability to support heart health and stabilize blood sugar levels. Meanwhile, polyunsaturated fats, particularly those omega-3 fatty acids in flaxseeds, walnuts, and fatty fish like salmon, are lauded for their direct role in combating inflammation.

It's crucial to integrate a variety of these fat sources into your diet. A practical approach might involve drizzling olive oil over your salads, snacking on nuts, or incorporating avocado into your meals. The aim is to make these healthy fats staple components of your pantry, ensuring they become a seamless part of your daily diet.

The Cost-Conscious Approach to Healthy Fats

A common concern is the perceived high cost associated with healthy eating, particularly when it comes to premium items like wild-caught salmon. However, embracing a diet rich in healthy fats doesn't have to strain your budget. Seeds such as chia, flaxseeds, and hemp offer budget-friendly sources of omega-3s. Likewise, purchasing nuts and olive oil in bulk can provide a cost-efficient way to incorporate healthy fats into your diet.

Furthermore, exploring the versatility of these ingredients can enhance your diet's variety without increasing your expenses. For instance, a simple change like using avocado as a butter substitute adds not just nutrition but a new flavor profile to your meals. Similarly, homemade dressings using olive oil as a base can replace store-bought versions that may contain unhealthy fats and additives.

The Sustainability of Healthy Fats in Your Diet

Adopting an anti-inflammatory diet is not a fleeting trend but a sustainable lifestyle change. To ensure the sustainability of incorporating healthy fats, it's essential to understand the 'why' behind your choices. Recognizing the anti-inflammatory and overall health benefits of these fats can transform your dietary changes from a task to a meaningful action towards better health.

3.3 Spices and Herbs that Pack an Anti-Inflammatory Punch

The science behind the anti-inflammatory effects of various spices and herbs is both fascinating and compelling. Many of these kitchen staples contain compounds that have been shown to possess anti-inflammatory properties, contributing to reduced risk of chronic diseases and improved well-being. The mechanisms through which these effects are achieved vary, from inhibiting inflammatory pathways to neutralizing free radicals. This section delves into how integrating these powerful botanicals into your diet can transform your health.

- **Turmeric: The Golden Wonder**

Turmeric, renowned for its vibrant hue and integral role in culinary traditions worldwide, stands out for its active compound, curcumin. Curcumin has been extensively studied for its powerful anti-inflammatory and antioxidant properties. Incorporating turmeric into your diet, however, requires a bit of know-how to ensure optimal absorption. Pairing it with black pepper, which contains piperine, significantly enhances curcumin's bioavailability, making this

combination a powerhouse in fighting inflammation.

- **Ginger: Spice with a Bite**

Ginger, with its distinctive fiery taste and aromatic qualities, is another hero in the anti-inflammatory arsenal. This root spice has been revered through ages and across cultures for its medicinal properties, including its ability to alleviate inflammatory conditions. Whether used fresh, dried, or powdered, ginger adds not just a kick to dishes but also contributes to your health by soothing inflammation and aiding in digestion.

- **Garlic: A Pungent Ally**

The pungent aroma and flavor of garlic have secured its place in kitchens around the globe. Beyond its culinary contributions, garlic is celebrated for its health benefits, including its capacity to support immune function and combat inflammation. Rich in sulfur-containing compounds such as allicin, garlic's therapeutic potential is unleashed when chopped, crushed, or minced, making it a simple yet potent addition to your anti-inflammatory diet.

- **Rosemary and Thyme: Fragrant Herbs with Robust Benefits**

Rosemary and thyme, with their aromatic appeal, are more than just culinary herbs. They are laden with anti-inflammatory compounds such as rosmarinic acid and thymol, respectively. Integrating these herbs into your cooking not only imparts delightful flavors but also imbues your meals with antioxidants that combat inflammation and support overall health.

A Practical Guide to Infusing Your Diet with Healing Flavors

Embracing the anti-inflammatory benefits of spices and herbs need not be complicated or costly. Start with incorporating turmeric into your morning smoothie or evening tea, adding a pinch of black pepper to enhance absorption. Experiment by adding ginger to stir-fries, soups, or even baking, for an invigorating flavor and health boost.

Garlic can transform a simple dish into a flavorful and healthful meal with just a few cloves. For maximum benefits, let chopped garlic sit for several minutes before cooking. Rosemary and thyme make excellent additions to roasted vegetables, meats, or homemade dressings, providing a burst of flavor and a dose of anti-inflammatory goodness.

3.4 Fermented Foods for Gut Health

The Role of Fermented Foods in Gut Health

Fermented foods have been a staple in human diets for millennia, historically valued for their preservation properties and their enriched flavors. Beyond these benefits, these foods are rich in probiotics—beneficial bacteria that inhabit our digestive tract. These microorganisms are allies in our wellness journey, supporting nutrient absorption, immune function, and even the production of anti-inflammatory compounds. By incorporating fermented foods into our diet, we provide these probiotic populations with the reinforcements needed to thrive and protect us.

Transforming Your Diet with Fermented Essentials

Integrating fermented foods into one's diet is both an art and a science. The variety is vast, from the tangy crunch of sauerkraut to the creamy, mild tartness of yogurt, each offering a unique profile of flavors and probiotic strains. Let's explore how to incorporate these nutrient powerhouses into your daily meals in a way that's both simple and pleasurable.

- **Sauerkraut and Kimchi: Crunchy Delights**

Sauerkraut and kimchi, fermented cabbage-based foods renowned for their digestive health benefits, are incredibly versatile. They can be enjoyed as a vibrant side dish, a flavorful topping on salads and sandwiches, or even straight from the jar. The key is to start with small servings to allow your gut to adjust to the influx of probiotics and gradually increase your intake.

Yogurt and kefir serve as excellent bases for smoothies, breakfast bowls, or as standalone snacks. Opt for plain, unsweetened varieties to avoid added sugars, which can counteract the anti-inflammatory benefits. For those sensitive to dairy, coconut yogurt and other plant-based alternatives offer a lactose-free way to enjoy these foods' probiotic and anti-inflammatory properties.

- **Yogurt and Kefir: Creamy Probiotic-Rich Foods**

- **Tempeh and Miso: Fermented Soy Delights**

Tempeh and miso bring not only depth of flavor to dishes but also a significant probiotic boost. Tempeh, a pressed soy product, makes for a hearty meat substitute, ideal for stir-fries and sandwiches. Miso, a fermented soybean paste, imparts a rich, umami flavor to soups, dressings, and marinades. Both are excellent diet additions for their gut health-supporting qualities.

Practical Tips for Integrating Fermented Foods

Embracing fermented foods means more than just sporadic consumption; it's about making them a consistent part of your diet. Start your day with a probiotic-rich smoothie incorporating yogurt or kefir. Incorporate sauerkraut or kimchi into your lunches and dinners as a flavorful, gut-healthy side. Use miso to enrich soups and sauces with probiotics and depth of flavor. Remember, heat can destroy the beneficial bacteria in fermented foods, so it's often best to add them at the end of the cooking process or incorporate them into cold dishes.

Chapter 4:

Breakfast Recipes to Kickstart Your Day

4.1 Antioxidant-Rich Smoothies

☐ Recipe 1: Berry Bliss Smoothie

Preparation time: 10 minutes
Servings: Serves 1
Mode of cooking: Blending

Ingredients: 1 cup mixed berries (blueberries, strawberries, raspberries) | 1 banana | 1 cup spinach | 1/2 cup unsweetened almond milk | 1 tablespoon chia seeds

Procedure: Combine the mixed berries, banana, spinach, almond milk, and chia seeds in a blender and blend on high until smooth. Pour into a glass and serve immediately for a nutrient-packed start to your day.

Nutritional values: 250 calories | 4g protein | 4g fats | 45g carbohydrates

☐ Recipe 2: Green Ginger Antioxidant Shake

Preparation time: 8 minutes
Servings: Serves 1
Mode of cooking: Blending

Ingredients: 1 cup kale | 1/2 apple, sliced | 1/2 inch ginger, peeled | 1 tablespoon flaxseeds | 1 cup coconut water

Procedure: Place kale, apple, ginger, flaxseeds, and coconut water in a blender and blend until smooth. Serve the refreshing shake immediately for a zesty and invigorating breakfast.

Nutritional values: 180 calories | 3g protein | 2g fats | 37g carbohydrates

⬜ Recipe 3: Tropical Turmeric Smoothie

Preparation time: 10 minutes
Servings: Serves 1
Mode of cooking: Blending

Ingredients: 1 cup pineapple chunks | 1/2 mango, peeled and cubed | 1/2 teaspoon turmeric powder | 1 tablespoon hemp seeds | 1 cup coconut milk

Procedure: Add pineapple, mango, turmeric powder, hemp seeds, and coconut milk to a blender and blend on high until smooth. The smoothie's vibrant color and flavors make it the perfect morning boost.

Nutritional values: 300 calories | 5g protein | 15g fats | 40g carbohydrates

⬜ Recipe 4: Red Beet Power Smoothie

Preparation time: 9 minutes
Servings: Serves 1
Mode of cooking: Blending

Ingredients: 1 small beet, peeled and chopped | 1/2 cup raspberries | 1/4 avocado | 1 cup water | 1 teaspoon honey (optional)

Procedure: Blend the beet, raspberries, avocado, water, and honey if you're including it, until everything is well combined and smooth. Enjoy this earthy and nutrient-dense drink to kickstart your day.

Nutritional values: 200 calories | 3g protein | 7g fats | 30g carbohydrates

☐ Recipe 5: Cinnamon Blueberry Wake-Up Shake

Preparation time: 7 minutes
Servings: Serves 1
Mode of cooking: Blending

4.2 Grain-Free Breakfast Bowls
☐ Recipe 1: Sunrise Berry Coconut Bowl.

Preparation time = 10 minutes
Servings = Serves 1
Mode of cooking = No cooking

Ingredients = 1 cup full-fat coconut yogurt | 1/2 cup mixed berries (strawberries, blueberries, raspberries) | 1/4 cup coconut flakes | 2 tablespoons pumpkin seeds | 1 tablespoon almond butter

Ingredients: 1 cup blueberries | 1/2 cup Greek yogurt | 1/4 teaspoon ground cinnamon | 1/2 banana | 1/2 cup oat milk

Procedure: In a blender, combine the blueberries, Greek yogurt, cinnamon, banana, and oat milk and process until the texture is creamy and smooth. This delicious smoothie is a perfect blend of protein, antioxidants, and spices.

Nutritional values: 220 calories | 10g protein | 3g fats | 40g carbohydrates

Procedure = Scoop the coconut yogurt into a serving bowl. Top with mixed berries and sprinkle coconut flakes and pumpkin seeds over the yogurt. Drizzle almond butter across the top for a creamy finish.

Nutritional values = 370 calories | 10g protein | 25g fat | 23g carbohydrates

☐ Recipe 2: Avocado Egg Boat Bowl.

Preparation time = 15 minutes
Servings = Serves 1
Mode of cooking = Baking

Ingredients = 1 avocado | 2 eggs | Pinch of salt | Pinch of black pepper | 1 tablespoon chopped chives

Procedure = Preheat the oven to 425°F (220°C). Slice the avocado in half and remove the pit, scoop out a bit of the flesh to make room for the egg. Crack an egg into each avocado half, season with salt and pepper, and place on a baking sheet. Bake for 15 minutes or until the egg whites are set. Sprinkle chopped chives on top before serving.

Nutritional values = 450 calories | 19g protein | 37g fat | 12g carbohydrates

☐ Recipe 3: Green Goodness Bowl.

Preparation time = 15 minutes
Servings = Serves 1
Mode of cooking = No cooking

Ingredients = 1 cup baby spinach | 1/4 cucumber, sliced | 1/4 cup shredded carrots | 1/2 small avocado, cubed | 2 tablespoons hemp hearts | Squeeze of lemon juice | Olive oil drizzle

Procedure = Place the baby spinach at the bottom of the bowl. Arrange the cucumber slices, shredded carrots, and avocado cubes on top of the spinach. Sprinkle hemp hearts over everything. Finish with a squeeze of fresh lemon juice and a drizzle of olive oil for dressing.

Nutritional values = 340 calories | 12g protein | 29g fat | 10g carbohydrates

Recipe 4: Mediterranean Tofu Scramble Bowl.

Preparation time = 20 minutes

Servings = Serves 1

Mode of cooking = Sautéing

Ingredients = 1/2 block firm tofu, crumbled | 2 tablespoons diced tomatoes | 2 tablespoons chopped spinach | 2 tablespoons diced red onions | 1 tablespoon olive oil | 1/4 teaspoon turmeric | Salt and pepper to taste

Procedure = Heat olive oil in a pan over medium heat. Add the crumbled tofu and turmeric, cooking and stirring for about 5 minutes. Mix in the tomatoes, spinach, and red onions, and continue to cook until vegetables are soft. Season with salt and pepper to taste. Serve hot.

Nutritional values = 250 calories | 18g protein | 15g fat | 10g carbohydrates

Recipe 5: Spicy Chicken Avocado Bowl.

Preparation time = 25 minutes

Servings = Serves 1

Mode of cooking = Grilling

Ingredients = 1 small chicken breast | 1/2 teaspoon paprika | Salt and pepper to taste | 1/2 avocado, sliced | 1/4 cup cucumber, diced | 1/4 cup cherry tomatoes, halved | Cilantro for garnish

Procedure = Season the chicken breast with paprika, salt, and pepper, and grill until fully cooked and juices run clear. Let the chicken rest for a few minutes, then slice it. In a bowl, arrange the avocado slices, cucumber, and cherry tomatoes. Add the sliced chicken on top and garnish with fresh cilantro.

Nutritional values = 410 calories | 35g protein | 25g fat | 9g carbohydrates

4.3 Protein-Packed Morning Mains

☐ Recipe 1: Turmeric Tofu Scramble

Preparation time = 15 minutes

Servings = Serves 2

Mode of cooking = Sautéing

Ingredients = 1 block firm tofu, drained and crumbled | 1 tsp turmeric | 1 tbsp olive oil | 1/2 cup diced bell peppers | 1/4 cup diced onions | 1 cup spinach leaves | Salt and pepper to taste

Procedure = Heat the olive oil in a non-stick pan over medium heat. Add the onions and bell peppers, sautéing until softened. Stir in the tofu and turmeric, cooking for about 5 minutes. Toss in the spinach and cook until wilted. Season with salt and pepper.

Nutritional values = 190 calories | 14g protein | 13g fat | 7g carbohydrates

☐ Recipe 2: Smoked Salmon Avocado Wrap

Preparation time = 10 minutes

Servings = Serves 1

Mode of cooking = No cooking

Ingredients = 1 large collard green leaf, stem removed | 3 oz smoked salmon | 1/2 avocado, sliced | 1/4 cup shredded carrots | 2 tbsp red onion, thinly sliced | 1 tbsp chopped dill

Procedure = Blanch the collard green leaf for 30 seconds to soften. Lay flat and arrange smoked salmon, avocado slices, shredded carrots, red onion, and dill in the center. Fold the leaf over the filling, tuck in the edges, and roll up tightly.

Nutritional values = 290 calories | 23g protein | 19g fat | 9g carbohydrates

☐ Recipe 3: Chia and Hemp Seed Pudding

Preparation time = 15 minutes (plus overnight soaking)

Servings = Serves 1

Mode of cooking = No cooking

Ingredients = 3 tbsp chia seeds | 1 tbsp hemp seeds | 1 cup unsweetened almond milk | 1/2 tsp vanilla extract | 1 tbsp almond butter | 1/4 cup blueberries

Procedure = In a bowl, combine chia seeds, hemp seeds, and almond milk. Stir in vanilla extract. Let the mixture sit overnight in the refrigerator. In the morning, top with almond butter and blueberries before serving.

Nutritional values = 340 calories | 12g protein | 24g fat | 21g carbohydrates

☐ Recipe 4: Spinach and Mushroom Egg Muffins

Preparation time = 20 minutes

Servings = Serves 3 (2 muffins each)

Mode of cooking = Baking

Ingredients = 6 eggs | 1 cup spinach, chopped | 1/2 cup mushrooms, diced | 1/4 cup red onion, diced | Salt and pepper to taste | 1 tbsp coconut oil (for greasing)

Procedure = Preheat the oven to 375°F (190°C). Whisk the eggs in a bowl and stir in the spinach, mushrooms, and red onions. Grease a muffin tin with coconut oil and pour the egg mixture into the cups. Bake for 15-20 minutes until set.

Nutritional values = 150 calories | 12g protein | 10g fat | 3g carbohydrates (per muffin)

☐ Recipe 5: Almond and Berry Breakfast Salad

Preparation time = 10 minutes

Servings = Serves 1

Mode of cooking = No cooking

Ingredients = 2 cups mixed greens | 1/2 cup fresh berries | 1/4 cup almonds, sliced | 2 tbsp extra-virgin olive oil | 1 tbsp lemon juice | Salt and pepper to taste

Procedure = In a large bowl, toss mixed greens, fresh berries, and sliced almonds. Whisk together extra-virgin olive oil, lemon juice, salt, and pepper to create a dressing. Drizzle the dressing over the salad just before serving.

Nutritional values = 250 calories | 5g protein | 20g fat | 14g carbohydrates

4.4 Anti-Inflammatory Baked Goods
☐ Recipe 1: Spiced Sweet Potato Muffins

Preparation time = 30 minutes

Servings = Serves 12

Mode of cooking = Baking

Ingredients = 2 cups almond flour | 1 tsp baking powder | 1/2 tsp sea salt | 1 tsp cinnamon | 1/2 tsp nutmeg | 3 eggs | 1 cup mashed sweet potato | 1/4 cup coconut oil, melted | 1/4 cup maple syrup | 1 tsp vanilla extract

Procedure = Preheat oven to 350°F (175°C). In a large bowl, mix almond flour, baking powder, salt, cinnamon, and nutmeg. In another bowl, whisk eggs, mashed sweet potato, coconut oil, maple syrup, and vanilla. Combine wet and dry ingredients until smooth. Divide batter into muffin tins and bake for 20-25 minutes.

Nutritional values = 190 calories | 6g protein | 12g fat | 15g carbohydrates

☐ *Recipe 2: Blueberry Oat Bars*

Preparation time = 35 minutes
Servings = Serves 8
Mode of cooking = Baking

Ingredients = 2 cups gluten-free oats | 1 tsp baking powder | 1/2 tsp salt | 1/2 cup unsweetened applesauce | 1/4 cup honey | 1 egg | 1 tsp vanilla extract | 1 cup fresh blueberries | 1/4 cup sliced almonds

Procedure = Preheat oven to 375°F (190°C). Mix oats, baking powder, and salt in a bowl. In another bowl, combine applesauce, honey, egg, and vanilla. Mix dry and wet ingredients, then fold in blueberries. Pour into a greased baking dish, sprinkle with almonds, and bake for 25-30 minutes.

Nutritional values = 180 calories | 5g protein | 4g fat | 32g carbohydrates

☐ *Recipe 3: Zucchini Bread with Flaxseeds*

Preparation time = 50 minutes
Servings = Serves 10
Mode of cooking = Baking

Ingredients = 1 1/2 cups whole wheat flour | 1/2 cup ground flaxseed | 1 tsp baking soda | 1/2 tsp salt | 1 tsp cinnamon | 1/2 cup honey | 1 egg | 1/3 cup olive oil | 1 tsp vanilla extract | 1 cup grated zucchini | 1/2 cup walnuts, chopped

Procedure = Preheat oven to 350°F (175°C). Mix flour, flaxseed, baking soda, salt, and cinnamon. In a separate bowl, beat together honey, egg, oil, and vanilla. Stir in zucchini and nuts.

Combine wet and dry ingredients. Pour into a loaf pan and bake for 45 minutes.

Nutritional values = 210 calories | 5g protein | 11g fat | 27g carbohydrates

Recipe 4: Ginger Pear Scones

Preparation time = 40 minutes
Servings = Serves 8
Mode of cooking = Baking

Ingredients = 2 cups spelt flour | 1/4 cup coconut sugar | 1 tbsp baking powder | 1/2 tsp salt | 1 tsp ground ginger | 1/4 cup cold coconut oil | 3/4 cup almond milk | 1 pear, diced

Procedure = Preheat oven to 400°F (200°C). Combine flour, coconut sugar, baking powder, salt, and ginger. Cut in coconut oil until mixture resembles coarse crumbs. Stir in almond milk until just moistened, then fold in pear. Drop scones onto a baking sheet and bake for 15-20 minutes.

Nutritional values = 220 calories | 4g protein | 10g fat | 32g carbohydrates

Recipe 5: Almond Butter Banana Cookies

Preparation time = 25 minutes
Servings = Serves 12
Mode of cooking = Baking

Ingredients = 2 ripe bananas, mashed | 1 cup almond butter | 1/2 cup coconut flour | 1/4 cup maple syrup | 1 tsp vanilla extract | 1/2 tsp cinnamon | 1/4 cup dark chocolate chips

Procedure = Preheat oven to 350°F (175°C). Mix bananas, almond butter, coconut flour, maple syrup, vanilla, and cinnamon until well combined. Fold in chocolate chips. Drop spoonfuls of the mixture onto a baking sheet and bake for 12-15 minutes.

Nutritional values = 200 calories | 6g protein | 12g fat | 20g carbohydrates

Chapter 5:

Inflammation-Fighting Salads & Soups

5.1 Fiber-Filled Salad Creations

☐ Recipe 1: Crunchy Kale and Chickpea Salad

Preparation time = 20 minutes

Servings = Serves 4

Mode of cooking = No cooking

Ingredients = 4 cups kale, ribs removed and leaves chopped | 1 can (15 oz) chickpeas, rinsed and drained | 1 red bell pepper, diced | 1/2 red onion, thinly sliced | 1/4 cup sunflower seeds | 2 tbsp extra-virgin olive oil | 1 lemon, juiced | 1 garlic clove, minced | Salt and pepper to taste

Procedure = In a large bowl, combine the kale, chickpeas, bell pepper, red onion, and sunflower seeds. In a small bowl, whisk together the olive oil, lemon juice, garlic, salt, and pepper to make the dressing. Pour the dressing over the salad and toss to coat evenly.

Nutritional values = 265 calories | 9g protein | 13g fat | 30g carbohydrates

☐ Recipe 2: Rainbow Quinoa and Veggie Salad

Preparation time = 25 minutes

Servings = Serves 3

Mode of cooking = Boiling

Ingredients = 1 cup quinoa | 1/2 cup cherry tomatoes, halved | 1/2 cucumber, diced | 1 yellow bell pepper, diced | 1

carrot, shredded | 1/4 cup fresh parsley, chopped | 3 tbsp extra-virgin olive oil | 2 tbsp apple cider vinegar | Salt and pepper to taste

Procedure = Cook quinoa according to package instructions and let it cool. In a large bowl, combine the cooled quinoa, tomatoes, cucumber, bell pepper, carrot, and parsley. For the dressing, whisk together olive oil, apple cider vinegar, salt, and pepper. Drizzle over the salad and toss well.

Nutritional values = 340 calories | 9g protein | 15g fat | 45g carbohydrates

☐ *Recipe 3: Spinach and Avocado Salad with Pomegranate*

Preparation time = 15 minutes
Servings = Serves 2
Mode of cooking = No cooking

Ingredients = 4 cups baby spinach | 1 avocado, diced | 1/2 cup pomegranate seeds | 1/4 cup walnuts, chopped | 1 tbsp flaxseed oil | 1 tbsp balsamic vinegar | Salt and pepper to taste

Procedure = Place the spinach in a large serving bowl and top with avocado, pomegranate seeds, and chopped walnuts. In a small bowl, whisk together flaxseed oil, balsamic vinegar, salt, and pepper to make the dressing. Drizzle the dressing over the salad before serving.

Nutritional values = 300 calories | 5g protein | 25g fat | 19g carbohydrates

☐ *Recipe 4: Broccoli and Bean Salad with Almond Dressing*

Preparation time = 20 minutes
Servings = Serves 4
Mode of cooking = Light Steaming/Blanching

Ingredients = 4 cups broccoli florets | 1 can (15 oz) white beans, rinsed and drained | 1/4 cup almonds, roughly chopped | 2 tbsp almond butter | 1 garlic clove, minced | 2 tbsp lemon juice | 2 tbsp water | Salt and pepper to taste

Procedure = Lightly steam the broccoli until it is bright green and tender. Quickly cool it in ice water to stop the cooking process. In a large bowl, mix the broccoli, white beans, and almonds. For the dressing, blend almond butter, garlic, lemon juice, water, salt, and pepper until smooth. Toss the salad with the dressing before serving.

Nutritional values = 255 calories | 14g protein | 9g fat | 33g carbohydrates

☐ Recipe 5: Mediterranean Artichoke and Tomato Salad

Preparation time = 20 minutes
Servings = Serves 4
Mode of cooking = No cooking

Ingredients = 2 cups mixed greens | 1 can (14 oz) artichoke hearts, drained and quartered | 1 cup cherry tomatoes, halved | 1/2 cup Kalamata olives, pitted and halved | 1/4 cup red onion, thinly sliced | 1/4 cup feta cheese, crumbled | 3 tbsp extra-virgin olive oil | 1 tbsp red wine vinegar | 1 tsp dried oregano | Salt and pepper to taste

Procedure = In a large bowl, combine the mixed greens, artichoke hearts, cherry tomatoes, Kalamata olives, and red onion. Sprinkle with crumbled feta cheese. For the dressing, whisk together olive oil, red wine vinegar, oregano, salt, and pepper. Drizzle the salad with the dressing and toss gently to coat.

Nutritional values = 220 calories | 5g protein | 18g fat | 12g carbohydrates

5.2 Gut-Soothing Soups and Stews

Recipe 1: Turmeric Ginger Carrot Soup

Preparation time = 40 minutes

Servings = Serves 4

Mode of cooking = Simmering

Ingredients = 1 tbsp coconut oil | 1 onion, chopped | 2 cloves garlic, minced | 2 tbsp fresh ginger, grated | 1 tbsp turmeric powder | 5 cups carrot, chopped | 4 cups vegetable broth | 1 can (14 oz) coconut milk | Salt and pepper to taste

Procedure = In a large pot, heat the coconut oil over medium heat. Add the onion and garlic, sautéing until soft. Stir in the ginger and turmeric, cooking for another minute. Add the carrots and vegetable broth, bringing to a boil before reducing to a simmer until carrots are tender. Blend the soup until smooth, then stir in coconut milk and season with salt and pepper. Warm through before serving.

Nutritional values = 250 calories | 3g protein | 18g fat | 22g carbohydrates

Recipe 2: Lentil and Kale Stew

Preparation time = 50 minutes

Servings = Serves 6

Mode of cooking = Simmering

Ingredients = 1 tbsp olive oil | 1 onion, diced | 2 carrots, diced | 2 stalks celery, diced | 3 cloves garlic, minced | 1 tsp cumin | 1 cup green lentils, rinsed | 6 cups vegetable broth | 2 cups kale, ribs removed and chopped | Salt and pepper to taste

Procedure = Heat olive oil in a large pot, adding onion, carrots, and celery to cook until softened. Stir in garlic and cumin, cooking for another minute. Add the lentils and vegetable broth, bringing to a simmer. Cover and cook until lentils are tender, about 35 minutes. Add kale in the last few minutes of cooking, allowing it to wilt. Season with salt and pepper to serve.

Nutritional values = 210 calories | 12g protein | 3g fat | 36g carbohydrates

☐ Recipe 3: Butternut Squash and Apple Soup

Preparation time = 45 minutes
Servings = Serves 4
Mode of cooking = Roasting and Blending

Ingredients = 1 medium butternut squash, peeled and cubed | 2 apples, peeled and chopped | 1 onion, diced | 2 tbsp olive oil | 4 cups vegetable broth | 1 tsp cinnamon | 1/2 tsp nutmeg | Salt and pepper to taste

Procedure = Toss the butternut squash, apples, and onion with olive oil and spread onto a baking sheet. Roast at 400°F (200°C) until everything is tender, about 25 minutes. Transfer the roasted vegetables and apples to a pot,

add vegetable broth, cinnamon, and nutmeg. Blend until smooth, season with salt and pepper, and heat through before serving.

Nutritional values = 180 calories | 2g protein | 7g fat | 31g carbohydrates

☐ Recipe 4: Gingery Mushroom and Barley Soup

Preparation time = 1 hour
Servings = Serves 6
Mode of cooking = Simmering

Ingredients = 1 tbsp sesame oil | 1 onion, chopped | 3 cloves garlic, minced | 2 inches fresh ginger, grated | 2 cups mushrooms, sliced | 1 cup pearl barley, rinsed | 6 cups vegetable broth | 2 tbsp soy sauce | 2 cups spinach | Salt and pepper to taste

Procedure = Heat the sesame oil in a large pot over medium heat. Add the onion, garlic, and ginger, sautéing until the onion is translucent. Add the mushrooms and cook until they begin to soften. Stir in the barley, vegetable broth, and soy sauce, bringing to a boil. Reduce the heat to simmer, cook until barley is tender, about 50 minutes. Stir in spinach until wilted. Adjust the seasoning with salt and pepper.

Nutritional values = 220 calories | 6g protein | 4g fat | 40g carbohydrates

☐ Recipe 5: Sweet Potato and Black Bean Chili

Preparation time = 45 minutes
Servings = Serves 6
Mode of cooking = Simmering

Ingredients = 1 tbsp avocado oil | 1 onion, diced | 2 cloves garlic, minced | 1 red bell pepper, diced | 2 sweet potatoes, peeled and cubed | 2 cans (15 oz each) black beans, rinsed and drained | 1 can (14.5 oz) diced tomatoes | 4 cups vegetable broth | 1 tbsp chili powder | 1 tsp cumin | Salt and pepper to taste

Procedure = In a large pot, heat the avocado oil over medium heat. Add onion, garlic, and red bell pepper, cooking until softened. Add the sweet potatoes, black beans, diced tomatoes, vegetable broth, chili powder, and cumin. Bring to a boil, then reduce to a simmer, cooking until the sweet potatoes are tender, about 30 minutes. Season with salt and pepper to taste.

Nutritional values = 295 calories | 10g protein | 3g fat | 57g carbohydrates

5.3 Dressings, Dips, and Toppings

Recipe 1: Avocado Cilantro Lime Dressing

Preparation time = 10 minutes

Servings = Serves 4

Mode of cooking = Blending

Ingredients = 1 ripe avocado | 1/4 cup cilantro leaves | 2 tbsp lime juice | 1 clove garlic | 1/4 cup water | Salt and pepper to taste

Procedure = Combine the avocado, cilantro, lime juice, garlic, and water in a blender. Blend until smooth, adding more water if needed to reach desired consistency. Season with salt and pepper to taste.

Nutritional values = 85 calories | 1g protein | 7g fat | 5g carbohydrates

Recipe 2: Turmeric Tahini Dip

Preparation time = 5 minutes

Servings = Serves 4

Mode of cooking = Mixing

Ingredients = 1/2 cup tahini | 1 tbsp turmeric powder | 1 clove garlic, minced | 2 tbsp lemon juice | Water, as needed | Salt to taste

Procedure = In a bowl, whisk together tahini, turmeric, garlic, and lemon juice. Gradually add water until the dip reaches your preferred consistency. Season with salt as needed.

Nutritional values = 180 calories | 5g protein | 16g fat | 8g carbohydrates

Recipe 3: Ginger Sesame Seed Topping

Preparation time = 10 minutes

Servings = Serves 6

Mode of cooking = Toasting

Ingredients = 1/4 cup sesame seeds | 1 tbsp finely grated ginger | 1 tsp coconut aminos | 1 tsp honey

Procedure = In a small pan, toast sesame seeds over medium heat until golden brown. Remove from heat and mix in grated ginger, coconut aminos, and honey. Stir until well combined.

Nutritional values = 45 calories | 2g protein | 3g fat | 3g carbohydrates

☐ Recipe 4: Zesty Lemon Herb Dressing

Preparation time = 5 minutes

Servings = Serves 4

Mode of cooking = Mixing

Ingredients = 1/4 cup olive oil | 1/4 cup lemon juice | 1 tbsp chopped fresh herbs (such as parsley, thyme, or basil) | 1 clove garlic, minced | Salt and pepper to taste

Procedure = In a jar, combine olive oil, lemon juice, fresh herbs, minced

garlic, salt, and pepper. Close the lid tightly and shake well until all ingredients are emulsified.

Nutritional values = 120 calories | 0g protein | 14g fat | 1g carbohydrates

☐ Recipe 5: Creamy Beet and Dill Dip

Preparation time = 15 minutes

Servings = Serves 4

Mode of cooking = Blending

Ingredients = 2 medium beets, cooked and peeled | 1/2 cup cashews, soaked for 2 hours and drained | 1 tbsp dill, chopped | 2 tbsp lemon juice | 1 clove garlic | Salt and pepper to taste

Procedure = In a blender, combine the cooked beets, soaked cashews, dill, lemon juice, and garlic. Blend until

smooth and creamy. Season with salt
and pepper to taste.

Nutritional values = 95 calories | 3g
protein | 7g fat | 8g carbohydrates

Chapter 6:

Nourishing Mains: Fish, Poultry & Vegetarian

6.1 Wild-Caught Fish and Seafood Dishes

☐ Recipe 1: Lemon and Dill Baked Salmon

Preparation time = 25 minutes

Servings = Serves 4

Mode of cooking = Baking

Ingredients = 4 wild-caught salmon fillets | 2 tbsp olive oil | 2 tbsp fresh dill, chopped | 1 lemon, sliced | Salt and pepper to taste

Procedure = Preheat the oven to 400°F (200°C). Place salmon on a baking sheet lined with parchment paper. Drizzle with olive oil and season with salt and pepper. Top each fillet with dill and lemon slices. Bake for 15-20 minutes, or until salmon flakes easily with a fork.

Nutritional values = 280 calories | 34g protein | 16g fat | 2g carbohydrates

☐ Recipe 2: Garlic Shrimp with Zucchini Noodles

Preparation time = 20 minutes

Servings = Serves 4

Mode of cooking = Sautéing

Ingredients = 1 lb large shrimp, peeled and deveined | 2 tbsp olive oil | 3 cloves garlic, minced | 4 zucchini, spiralized | Salt and pepper to taste | Red pepper flakes (optional)

Procedure = Heat olive oil in a large skillet over medium heat. Add garlic and sauté until fragrant, about 1 minute. Add shrimp and cook until pink, about 2-3 minutes per side. Season with salt, pepper, and red pepper flakes if using. Toss in spiralized zucchini and cook for an additional 2 minutes. Serve immediately.

Nutritional values = 210 calories | 28g protein | 8g fat | 8g carbohydrates

☐ *Recipe 3: Herb Crusted Cod with Roasted Vegetables*

Preparation time = 40 minutes
Servings = Serves 4
Mode of cooking = Baking and Roasting

Ingredients = 4 cod fillets | 2 tbsp olive oil | 1 tbsp rosemary, chopped | 1 tbsp thyme, chopped | Salt and pepper to taste | 2 cups mixed vegetables (e.g., bell peppers, zucchini, cherry tomatoes)

Procedure = Preheat oven to 400°F (200°C). Toss the mixed vegetables with half the olive oil and season with salt and pepper. Spread on a baking sheet and roast for 20 minutes. Combine the herbs with the remaining olive oil. Season the cod with salt and pepper, and coat with the herb mixture. Place the cod on the roasting vegetables and bake for 15-20 minutes, or until the cod is cooked through.

Nutritional values = 240 calories | 27g protein | 10g fat | 8g carbohydrates

☐ *Recipe 4: Spicy Grilled Mackerel*

Preparation time = 25 minutes
Servings = Serves 4
Mode of cooking = Grilling

Ingredients = 4 mackerel fillets | 2 tbsp olive oil | 1 tsp paprika | 1/2 tsp cayenne pepper | 1 lemon, juiced | Salt to taste

Procedure = Preheat grill to medium-high. Mix olive oil, paprika, cayenne pepper, lemon juice, and salt in a bowl. Brush the mixture over the mackerel fillets. Grill for 4-5 minutes on each side, or until the fish is opaque and flaky. Serve with lemon wedges.

Nutritional values = 290 calories | 22g protein | 20g fat | 1g carbohydrates

Recipe 5: Baked Trout with Almonds

Preparation time = 30 minutes
Servings = Serves 4
Mode of cooking = Baking

Ingredients = 4 whole trout, cleaned and gutted | 2 tbsp olive oil | 1/4 cup almonds, sliced | 2 tbsp parsley, chopped | Salt and pepper to taste | Lemon slices, for garnish

Procedure = Preheat oven to 375°F (190°C). Brush the trout with olive oil inside and out, and season with salt and pepper. Place trout in a baking dish and sprinkle with sliced almonds and parsley. Bake for 20-25 minutes, or until the trout is cooked through and almonds are golden. Serve garnished with lemon slices.

Nutritional values = 310 calories | 31g protein | 18g fat | 3g carbohydrates

Recipe 6: Seared Scallops with Spinach

Preparation time = 20 minutes
Servings = Serves 4
Mode of cooking = Searing

Ingredients = 1 lb sea scallops | 2 tbsp olive oil | Salt and pepper to taste | 4 cups spinach | 1 clove garlic, minced

Procedure = Heat olive oil in a large skillet over high heat. Season scallops with salt and pepper. Sear scallops on each side for 1-2 minutes, until a golden crust forms. Remove scallops and lower the heat to medium. Add garlic and spinach to the skillet and cook until wilted. Serve scallops over the spinach.

Nutritional values = 180 calories | 20g protein | 10g fat | 3g carbohydrates

Recipe 7: Lemon Pepper Tuna Steak

Preparation time = 15 minutes

Servings = Serves 4

Mode of cooking = Grilling

Ingredients = 4 tuna steaks | 2 tbsp olive oil | 1 tbsp lemon pepper seasoning

Procedure = Preheat grill to high heat. Brush both sides of the tuna steaks with olive oil and season with lemon pepper seasoning. Grill for 2-3 minutes on each side for medium-rare, or to desired doneness.

Nutritional values = 230 calories | 40g protein | 5g fat | 0g carbohydrates

Recipe 8: Mediterranean-Style Baked Haddock

Preparation time = 30 minutes

Servings = Serves 4

Mode of cooking = Baking

Ingredients = 4 haddock fillets | 2 tbsp olive oil | 1 tomato, sliced | 1/4 cup Kalamata olives, sliced | 1 tbsp capers | 1 tsp dried oregano | Salt and pepper to taste

Procedure = Preheat oven to 375°F (190°C). Place the haddock in a baking dish and drizzle with olive oil. Top with tomato slices, olives, capers, and oregano. Season with salt and pepper. Bake for 20-25 minutes, or until fish flakes easily with a fork.

Nutritional values = 200 calories | 23g protein | 10g fat | 3g carbohydrates

Recipe 9: Asian-Style Grilled Tilapia

Preparation time = 20 minutes + marinating
Servings = Serves 4
Mode of cooking = Grilling

Ingredients = 4 tilapia fillets | 2 tbsp soy sauce (or tamari for gluten-free) | 1 tbsp sesame oil | 1 clove garlic, minced | 1 inch ginger, minced | 1 tbsp honey | Sesame seeds, for garnish

Procedure = Mix soy sauce, sesame oil, garlic, ginger, and honey in a bowl. Marinate the tilapia fillets in the mixture for at least 30 minutes. Preheat grill to medium heat and oil the grates. Grill tilapia for 3-4 minutes on each side or until cooked through. Garnish with sesame seeds before serving.

Nutritional values = 160 calories | 23g protein | 4g fat | 7g carbohydrates

6.2 Lean Poultry Recipes

☐ Recipe 10: Herb Roasted Salmon with Tomatoes

Preparation time = 20 minutes
Servings = Serves 4
Mode of cooking = Roasting

Ingredients = 4 wild-caught salmon fillets | 2 tbsp olive oil | 1 tbsp mixed dried herbs (e.g., basil, oregano, thyme) | 1 cup cherry tomatoes | Salt and pepper to taste

Procedure = Preheat oven to 400°F (200°C). Place salmon on a baking sheet and drizzle with olive oil. Season with mixed herbs, salt, and pepper. Scatter cherry tomatoes around the salmon. Roast for 12-15 minutes, or until salmon is cooked through and tomatoes are blistered.

Nutritional values = 270 calories | 35g protein | 14g fat | 3g carbohydrates

☐ Recipe 1: Herbed Grilled Chicken Breast

Preparation time = 20 minutes
Servings = Serves 4
Mode of cooking = Grilling

Ingredients = 4 boneless, skinless chicken breasts | 2 tbsp olive oil | 1 tsp dried oregano | 1 tsp dried basil | 1/2 tsp garlic powder | 1/2 tsp paprika | Salt and pepper to taste

Procedure = Preheat grill to medium-high heat. Pound chicken breasts to even thickness. Combine olive oil, oregano, basil, garlic powder, paprika, salt, and pepper. Brush mixture onto both sides of chicken breasts. Grill for 6-7 minutes per side until internal temperature reaches 165°F.

Nutritional values = 220 calories | 30g protein | 10g fat | 1g carbohydrates

☐ Recipe 2: Turmeric Chicken Stir-Fry

Preparation time = 30 minutes
Servings = Serves 4
Mode of cooking = Stir-frying

Ingredients = 1 lb chicken breast, thinly sliced | 2 tbsp coconut oil | 1 tsp ground turmeric | 1 bell pepper, julienned | 1 onion, thinly sliced | 2 cloves garlic, minced | 1 tbsp ginger, minced | Salt and pepper to taste

Procedure = Heat coconut oil in a wok over medium-high heat. Add chicken, turmeric, salt, and pepper, cooking until chicken is browned. Remove chicken and set aside. In the same wok, stir-fry bell pepper, onion, garlic, and ginger until vegetables are tender. Return chicken to the wok, mixing well with vegetables. Cook for an additional 3 minutes.

Nutritional values = 240 calories | 26g protein | 14g fat | 7g carbohydrates

☐ Recipe 3: Lemon Garlic Roasted Chicken Thighs

Preparation time = 60 minutes

Servings = Serves 4

Mode of cooking = Roasting

Ingredients = 4 chicken thighs | 1 tbsp olive oil | 3 cloves garlic, minced | 1 lemon, juiced and zested | 1 tsp dried thyme | Salt and pepper to taste

Procedure = Preheat oven to 400°F (200°C). Rub chicken thighs with olive oil, garlic, lemon juice, zest, thyme, salt, and pepper. Arrange in a baking dish and roast for 45 minutes, or until skin is crispy and internal temperature is 165°F.

Nutritional values = 300 calories | 24g protein | 20g fat | 3g carbohydrates

☐ Recipe 4: Balsamic Glazed Chicken

Preparation time = 25 minutes

Servings = Serves 4

Mode of cooking = Sautéing

Ingredients = 4 boneless, skinless chicken breasts | 2 tbsp balsamic vinegar | 1 tbsp olive oil | 1 clove garlic, minced | 1 tsp dried rosemary | Salt and pepper to taste | Fresh parsley for garnish

Procedure = Heat olive oil in a skillet over medium heat. Season chicken with salt, pepper, and rosemary. Cook until golden, about 4 minutes each side. Reduce heat to low, add balsamic vinegar and garlic, coating the chicken well. Cover and simmer until cooked through. Garnish with parsley.

Nutritional values = 210 calories | 31g protein | 7g fat | 4g carbohydrates

🞏 Recipe 5: Spicy Paprika Chicken Drumsticks

Preparation time = 40 minutes
Servings = Serves 4
Mode of cooking = Baking

Ingredients = 8 chicken drumsticks | 2 tbsp olive oil | 1 tbsp smoked paprika | 1/2 tsp cayenne pepper | 1 tsp garlic powder | Salt and pepper to taste

Procedure = Preheat oven to 425°F (220°C). Mix olive oil, smoked paprika, cayenne pepper, garlic powder, salt, and pepper. Coat drumsticks evenly with the spice mixture. Arrange on a baking sheet and bake for 35 minutes or until the internal temperature is 165°F.

Nutritional values = 280 calories | 24g protein | 18g fat | 1g carbohydrates

🞏 Recipe 6: Cilantro Lime Chicken Skewers

Preparation time = 25 minutes + marinating
Servings = Serves 4
Mode of cooking = Grilling

Ingredients = 1 lb chicken breast, cubed | 1/4 cup fresh cilantro, chopped | 2 tbsp olive oil | 1 lime, juiced | 1 clove garlic, minced | Salt and pepper to taste | Wooden skewers

Procedure = Soak wooden skewers in water for 30 minutes. Marinate chicken with cilantro, olive oil, lime juice, garlic, salt, and pepper for at least 1 hour. Preheat grill to medium-high heat. Thread chicken onto skewers and grill for about 5 minutes on each side.

Nutritional values = 230 calories | 35g protein | 9g fat | 2g carbohydrates

☐ *Recipe 7: Sage and Thyme Chicken Breast*

Preparation time = 30 minutes

Servings = Serves 4

Mode of cooking = Sautéing

Ingredients = 4 boneless, skinless chicken breasts | 2 tbsp olive oil | 1 tsp dried sage | 1 tsp dried thyme | Salt and pepper to taste

Procedure = Pound chicken breasts to even thickness. Heat olive oil in a skillet over medium heat. Season chicken with sage, thyme, salt, and pepper. Cook for 5-7 minutes each side until golden and cooked through.

Nutritional values = 220 calories | 30g protein | 10g fat | 0g carbohydrates

☐ *Recipe 8: Mustard Glazed Chicken Tenders*

Preparation time = 20 minutes

Servings = Serves 4

Mode of cooking = Baking

Ingredients = 1 lb chicken tenders | 1 tbsp Dijon mustard | 2 tbsp olive oil | 1 tsp honey | 1 tsp apple cider vinegar | Salt and pepper to taste

Procedure = Preheat oven to 375°F (190°C). Mix Dijon mustard, olive oil, honey, vinegar, salt, and pepper. Coat chicken tenders in the mustard mixture and arrange on a baking sheet. Bake for 15 minutes or until chicken is cooked through.

Nutritional values = 210 calories | 29g protein | 9g fat | 3g carbohydrates

☐ Recipe 9: Ground Turkey and Kale Skillet

Preparation time = 30 minutes

Servings = Serves 4

Mode of cooking = Skillet cooking

Ingredients = 1 lb ground turkey | 1 tbsp olive oil | 2 cups kale, chopped | 1 onion, diced | 2 cloves garlic, minced | Salt and pepper to taste | Red pepper flakes (optional)

Procedure = Heat olive oil in a skillet over medium heat. Add ground turkey and cook until browned. Add onion and garlic; cook until soft. Stir in kale, cooking until wilted. Season with salt, pepper, and red pepper flakes if desired.

Nutritional values = 250 calories | 27g protein | 13g fat | 7g carbohydrates

☐ Recipe 10: Lemon Rosemary Chicken

Preparation time = 35 minutes

Servings = Serves 4

Mode of cooking = Roasting

Ingredients = 4 boneless, skinless chicken breasts | 2 tbsp olive oil | 2 lemons, 1 juiced and 1 sliced | 1 tbsp fresh rosemary, chopped | Salt and pepper to taste

Procedure = Preheat oven to 375°F (190°C). Season chicken with salt and pepper. Mix the olive oil, lemon juice, and rosemary and rub on the chicken. Place slices of lemon on top of the chicken. Roast for 25-30 minutes or until the internal temperature is 165°F.

Nutritional values = 220 calories | 31g protein | 9g fat | 2g carbohydrates

6.3 Plant-Based Protein-Rich Meals

□ Recipe 1: Spicy Black Bean and Quinoa Salad

Preparation time = 20 minutes
Servings = Serves 4
Mode of cooking = No-cook

Ingredients = 1 cup cooked quinoa | 1 can black beans, rinsed and drained | 1 red bell pepper, chopped | 1/2 red onion, finely chopped | 1/2 cup cilantro, chopped | 1 avocado, diced | 2 tbsp lime juice | 1 tbsp olive oil | 1 tsp cumin | 1/2 tsp chili powder | Salt and pepper to taste

Procedure = In a large bowl, mix the quinoa, black beans, bell pepper, onion, and cilantro. In a small bowl, whisk together lime juice, olive oil, cumin, chili powder, salt, and pepper to make the dressing. Pour the dressing over the salad and toss well. Gently fold in the diced avocado just before serving.

Nutritional values = 285 calories | 11g protein | 9g fat | 45g carbohydrates

□ Recipe 2: Mediterranean Chickpea Stew

Preparation time = 35 minutes
Servings = Serves 4
Mode of cooking = Simmering

Ingredients = 1 tbsp olive oil | 1 onion, diced | 2 cloves garlic, minced | 2 carrots, diced | 1 can chickpeas, drained and rinsed | 1 can diced tomatoes | 2 cups vegetable broth | 1 tsp dried oregano | 1 tsp dried basil | Salt and pepper to taste | 2 cups spinach

Procedure = Heat olive oil in a large pot over medium heat. Add onion and garlic, cooking until onion is translucent. Stir in carrots and cook for an additional 5 minutes. Add chickpeas, tomatoes, vegetable broth, oregano, and basil. Bring to a boil, then reduce heat and simmer for 20 minutes. Stir in spinach just before serving and season with salt and pepper.

Nutritional values = 256 calories | 8g protein | 5g fat | 44g carbohydrates

☐ Recipe 3: Tofu and Broccoli Stir-Fry

Preparation time = 25 minutes
Servings = Serves 4
Mode of cooking = Stir-frying

Ingredients = 14 oz firm tofu, pressed and cubed | 2 tbsp sesame oil | 2 cups broccoli florets | 1 red bell pepper, sliced | 2 tbsp soy sauce | 1 tbsp ginger, minced | 1 clove garlic, minced | Salt and pepper to taste | Sesame seeds for garnish

Procedure = Heat sesame oil in a wok over medium-high heat. Add tofu and stir-fry until golden brown, about 5 minutes. Remove tofu and set aside. In the same wok, add broccoli and bell pepper, stir-frying for about 3 minutes. Add ginger and garlic, cooking for another 2 minutes. Return tofu to the wok, add soy sauce, and season with salt and pepper. Stir well to combine. Garnish with sesame seeds before serving.

Nutritional values = 220 calories | 15g protein | 12g fat | 15g carbohydrates

☐ Recipe 4: Lentil and Spinach Soup

Preparation time = 45 minutes
Servings = Serves 4
Mode of cooking = Simmering

Ingredients = 1 tbsp olive oil | 1 onion, chopped | 2 cloves garlic, minced | 1 carrot, chopped | 1 stalk celery, chopped | 1 cup dried lentils, rinsed | 4 cups vegetable stock | 1 tsp turmeric | 1 tsp cumin | Salt and pepper to taste | 2 cups spinach leaves

Procedure = Heat olive oil in a large pot over medium heat. Add onion, garlic, carrot, and celery and cook until softened, about 5 minutes. Add lentils, vegetable stock, turmeric, cumin, salt, and pepper. Bring to a boil, then reduce heat and simmer for 30 minutes, or until lentils are tender. Stir in spinach and cook until wilted, about 3 minutes.

Nutritional values = 230 calories | 14g protein | 4g fat | 35g carbohydrates

☐ Recipe 5: Stuffed Bell Peppers with Quinoa and Mushrooms

Preparation time = 50 minutes
Servings = Serves 4
Mode of cooking = Baking

Ingredients = 4 bell peppers, tops cut off and seeded | 1 tbsp olive oil | 1 onion, finely chopped | 2 cloves garlic, minced | 1 cup mushrooms, chopped | 1 cup cooked quinoa | 1 tbsp balsamic vinegar | 1/4 cup pine nuts | Salt and pepper to taste

Procedure = Preheat oven to 375°F (190°C). Heat olive oil in a skillet over medium heat. Add onion and garlic, cooking until softened. Add mushrooms and cook until browned. Remove from heat, then stir in cooked quinoa, balsamic vinegar, and pine nuts. Season with salt and pepper. Stuff the bell peppers with the quinoa mixture and place in a baking dish. Bake for 30 minutes, or until the peppers are tender.

Nutritional values = 265 calories | 8g protein | 10g fat | 38g carbohydrates

☐ Recipe 6: Vegan Chili

Preparation time = 40 minutes
Servings = Serves 4
Mode of cooking = Simmering

Ingredients = 1 tbsp olive oil | 1 onion, diced | 2 cloves garlic, minced | 1 carrot, diced | 1 bell pepper, diced | 1 zucchini, diced | 1 can kidney beans, drained and rinsed | 1 can black beans, drained and rinsed | 2 cups tomato sauce | 1 cup vegetable broth | 1 tbsp chili powder | 1 tsp cumin | Salt and pepper to taste

Procedure = Heat olive oil in a large pot over medium heat. Add onion, garlic, carrot, and bell pepper, cooking until vegetables are soft. Add zucchini, kidney beans, black beans, tomato sauce, vegetable broth, chili powder, and cumin. Bring to a boil, then reduce heat and simmer for 25 minutes. Season with salt and pepper to taste.

Nutritional values = 295 calories | 14g protein | 4g fat | 54g carbohydrates

☐ *Recipe 7: Curried Cauliflower Rice*

Preparation time = 20 minutes
Servings = Serves 4
Mode of cooking = Sautéing

Ingredients = 1 head cauliflower, grated into rice-sized pieces | 1 tbsp coconut oil | 1 onion, diced | 1 tbsp curry powder | 1/2 cup peas | 1/2 cup carrots, diced | Salt and pepper to taste

Procedure = Heat coconut oil in a large skillet over medium heat. Add onion and cook until translucent. Stir in curry powder, cooking for another minute until fragrant. Add cauliflower,

peas, and carrots, cooking for about 10 minutes or until vegetables are tender. Season with salt and pepper.

Nutritional values = 120 calories | 4g protein | 7g fat | 13g carbohydrates

☐ *Recipe 8: Sweet Potato and Black Bean Tacos*

Preparation time = 30 minutes
Servings = Serves 4
Mode of cooking = Baking

Ingredients = 2 large sweet potatoes, peeled and diced | 1 tbsp olive oil | 1 tsp smoked paprika | Salt and pepper to taste | 1 can black beans, rinsed and drained | 8 small corn tortillas | 1 avocado, sliced | 1/4 cup fresh cilantro, chopped

Procedure = Preheat oven to 400°F (200°C). Toss sweet potatoes with olive oil, smoked paprika, salt, and pepper. Spread on a baking sheet and roast for 20 minutes, or until tender. Warm the black beans and tortillas. Assemble tacos with sweet potatoes, black beans, avocado slices, and cilantro.

Nutritional values = 350 calories | 8g protein | 10g fat | 58g carbohydrates

☐ Recipe 9: Spinach and Artichoke Stuffed Portobellos

Preparation time = 30 minutes
Servings = Serves 4
Mode of cooking = Baking

Ingredients = 4 large portobello mushrooms, stems and gills removed | 1 tbsp olive oil | 1 cup artichoke hearts, chopped | 2 cups spinach, chopped | 1/2 cup almond ricotta | Salt and pepper to taste

Procedure = Preheat oven to 375°F (190°C). Brush mushrooms with olive oil and place on a baking sheet. In a skillet, sauté artichoke hearts and spinach until spinach is wilted. Remove from heat, stir in almond ricotta, and season with salt

and pepper. Fill mushrooms with the spinach mixture. Bake for 20 minutes or until mushrooms are tender.

Nutritional values = 180 calories | 7g protein | 8g fat | 20g carbohydrates

☐ Recipe 10: Moroccan Spiced Lentil Soup

Preparation time = 45 minutes
Servings = Serves 4
Mode of cooking = Simmering

Ingredients = 1 tbsp olive oil | 1 onion, chopped | 2 cloves garlic, minced | 2 carrots, diced | 2 tsp Moroccan spice blend | 1 cup dried lentils | 4 cups vegetable broth | 1 can diced tomatoes | Salt and pepper to taste | Fresh parsley for garnish

Procedure = Heat olive oil in a large pot over medium heat. Add onion and garlic, cooking until onion is translucent. Add carrots and Moroccan spice blend, cooking for another 2 minutes. Stir in lentils, vegetable broth, and diced tomatoes. Bring to a boil, then reduce heat and simmer for 30 minutes or until lentils are tender. Season with

salt and pepper. Garnish with fresh
parsley before serving.

Nutritional values = 235 calories |
13g protein | 3g fat | 40g carbohydrates

Chapter 7:

Sides, Snacks & Sweets

7.1 Anti-Inflammatory Sauces and Dressings

☐ Recipe 1: Turmeric Ginger Dressing

Preparation time = 10 minutes
Servings = Serves 6
Mode of cooking = No-cook

Ingredients = 1/4 cup olive oil | 1/4 cup apple cider vinegar | 1 tbsp fresh ginger, grated | 1 tsp turmeric | 1 clove garlic, minced | 1 tbsp honey | Salt and pepper to taste

Procedure = Combine olive oil, apple cider vinegar, ginger, turmeric, garlic, and honey in a blender. Blend until smooth. Season with salt and pepper to taste. Store in an airtight container in the refrigerator.

Nutritional values = 120 calories | 0g protein | 11g fat | 4g carbohydrates

☐ Recipe 2: Avocado Cilantro Lime Dressing

Preparation time = 10 minutes
Servings = Serves 8
Mode of cooking = No-cook

Ingredients = 1 ripe avocado | 1/4 cup cilantro, chopped | Juice of 2 limes | 1/4 cup olive oil | 1 clove garlic | Salt and pepper to taste

Procedure = Place avocado, cilantro, lime juice, olive oil, and garlic in a food processor or blender. Blend until smooth and creamy. Add a bit of water if necessary to reach desired consistency. Season with salt and pepper to taste.

Nutritional values = 105 calories | 1g protein | 10g fat | 3g carbohydrates

☐ *Recipe 3: Anti-Inflammatory Basil Pesto*

Preparation time = 15 minutes
Servings = Serves 10
Mode of cooking = No-cook

Ingredients = 2 cups fresh basil leaves | 1/3 cup walnuts | 2 cloves garlic | 1/2 cup extra virgin olive oil | Juice of 1 lemon | Salt to taste

Procedure = Place basil, walnuts, and garlic in a food processor and pulse until roughly chopped. Gradually add olive oil and lemon juice while continuing to

blend until desired consistency is reached. Season with salt.

Nutritional values = 140 calories | 2g protein | 14g fat | 2g carbohydrates

☐ *Recipe 4: Ginger Tahini Sauce*

Preparation time = 10 minutes
Servings = Serves 8
Mode of cooking = No-cook

Ingredients = 1/2 cup tahini | 1/4 cup water | 2 tbsp lemon juice | 1 tbsp grated ginger | 1 clove garlic, minced | Salt to taste

Procedure = Whisk together tahini, water, lemon juice, ginger, and garlic in a bowl until smooth. Add more water if necessary to reach a pourable consistency. Season with salt to taste.

Nutritional values = 110 calories | 4g protein | 9g fat | 3g carbohydrates

Recipe 5: Sweet Red Pepper and Walnut Dip

Preparation time = 15 minutes

Servings = Serves 8

Mode of cooking = No-cook

Ingredients = 1 roasted red bell pepper | 1 cup walnuts | 1 clove garlic | 2 tbsp olive oil | 1 tsp smoked paprika | Salt to taste

Procedure = Blend roasted red bell pepper, walnuts, garlic, olive oil, and smoked paprika in a food processor until smooth. Transfer to a serving bowl and season with salt to taste.

Nutritional values = 100 calories | 2g protein | 9g fat | 3g carbohydrates

7.2 Veggie-Centric Side Dishes
Recipe 1: Garlic Roasted Brussels Sprouts

Preparation time = 30 minutes

Servings = Serves 4

Mode of cooking = Roasting

Ingredients = 1 lb Brussels sprouts, halved | 3 tbsp olive oil | 4 cloves garlic, minced | Salt and pepper to taste

Procedure = Preheat the oven to 400°F (200°C). Toss Brussels sprouts with olive oil and garlic on a baking sheet. Season with salt and pepper. Roast for 20-25 minutes, or until caramelized and tender, stirring occasionally.

Nutritional values = 150 calories | 4g protein | 10g fat | 13g carbohydrates

☐ Recipe 2: Ginger Turmeric Cauliflower Rice

Preparation time = 20 minutes
Servings = Serves 4
Mode of cooking = Sautéing

Ingredients = 1 head cauliflower, grated | 1 tbsp coconut oil | 1 tsp ginger, minced | 1 tsp turmeric | Salt and pepper to taste

Procedure = Heat coconut oil in a large skillet. Add ginger and turmeric, sauté for 1 minute. Add grated cauliflower, season with salt and pepper, and cook for 5-7 minutes until soft and golden.

Nutritional values = 77 calories | 3g protein | 4g fat | 9g carbohydrates

☐ Recipe 3: Balsamic Glazed Carrots

Preparation time = 25 minutes
Servings = Serves 4
Mode of cooking = Glazing

Ingredients = 1 lb carrots, peeled and sliced | 2 tbsp balsamic vinegar | 1 tbsp olive oil | 1 tbsp honey | Salt and pepper to taste

Procedure = Preheat the oven to 400°F (200°C). Toss carrots with olive oil, honey, and balsamic vinegar on a baking sheet. Season with salt and pepper. Roast for 20 minutes, or until tender.

Nutritional values = 123 calories | 1g protein | 4g fat | 21g carbohydrates

Recipe 4: Lemon Garlic Steamed Asparagus

Preparation time = 15 minutes

Servings = Serves 4

Mode of cooking = Steaming

Ingredients = 1 lb asparagus, trimmed | 1 tbsp olive oil | 2 cloves garlic, minced | Juice of 1 lemon | Salt and pepper to taste

Procedure = Steam asparagus until tender, about 3-5 minutes. Meanwhile, heat olive oil in a pan, add garlic and cook until fragrant. Remove from heat, stir in lemon juice. Pour over asparagus, season with salt and pepper to taste.

Nutritional values = 69 calories | 3g protein | 5g fat | 5g carbohydrates

Recipe 5: Spiced Roasted Sweet Potatoes

Preparation time = 35 minutes

Servings = Serves 4

Mode of cooking = Roasting

Ingredients = 2 large sweet potatoes, cubed | 2 tbsp olive oil | 1 tsp paprika | 1/2 tsp cinnamon | Salt and pepper to taste

Procedure = Preheat the oven to 425°F (220°C). Toss sweet potatoes with olive oil, paprika, and cinnamon on a baking sheet. Season with salt and pepper. Roast for 25-30 minutes, or until crisp and tender, stirring occasionally.

Nutritional values = 162 calories | 2g protein | 7g fat | 24g carbohydrates

7.3 Guilt-Free Desserts & Treats

☐ Recipe 1: Avocado Chocolate Mousse

Preparation time = 15 minutes
Servings = Serves 4
Mode of cooking = Blending

Ingredients = 2 ripe avocados | 1/4 cup cocoa powder | 1/4 cup maple syrup | 1 tsp vanilla extract | Pinch of salt

Procedure = Blend avocados, cocoa powder, maple syrup, vanilla extract, and a pinch of salt in a food processor until smooth. Refrigerate for at least 1 hour before serving.

Nutritional values = 230 calories | 3g protein | 15g fat | 28g carbohydrates

☐ Recipe 2: Coconut Almond Energy Balls

Preparation time = 20 minutes
Servings = Serves 12 balls
Mode of cooking = No-cook

Ingredients = 1 cup dates, pitted | 1/2 cup almonds | 1/2 cup shredded coconut | 1 tbsp chia seeds | 1 tsp vanilla extract

Procedure = Process dates, almonds, shredded coconut, chia seeds, and vanilla extract in a food processor until the mixture sticks together. Roll into balls and refrigerate to set.

Nutritional values = 100 calories | 2g protein | 5g fat | 14g carbohydrates

☐ Recipe 3: Baked Apple Cinnamon Chips

Preparation time = 2 hours
Servings = Serves 4
Mode of cooking = Baking

Ingredients = 2 apples, thinly sliced | 1 tsp cinnamon | 1 tbsp maple syrup

Procedure = Preheat oven to 200°F (93°C). Arrange apple slices on a baking sheet lined with parchment paper. Mix cinnamon and maple syrup, brush over apples. Bake for 2 hours until crispy.

Nutritional values = 77 calories | 0g protein | 0g fat | 20g carbohydrates

☐ Recipe 4: Berry Coconut Yogurt Parfait

Preparation time = 10 minutes
Servings = Serves 4
Mode of cooking = Layering

Ingredients = 2 cups coconut yogurt | 1 cup mixed berries (fresh or frozen) | 1/4 cup granola | 2 tbsp honey

Procedure = Layer coconut yogurt, mixed berries, and granola in serving glasses. Drizzle with honey before serving.

Nutritional values = 150 calories | 4g protein | 6g fat | 22g carbohydrates

☐ Recipe 5: Dark Chocolate Pumpkin Seed Bark

Preparation time = 15 minutes + chilling
Servings = Serves 8
Mode of cooking = Melting and chilling

Ingredients = 200g dark chocolate (70% or higher) | 1/2 cup pumpkin seeds | 1/4 tsp sea salt

Procedure = Melt dark chocolate in a double boiler or microwave. Stir in pumpkin seeds and spread mixture on a baking sheet lined with parchment paper. Sprinkle with sea salt. Chill until set, then break into pieces.

Nutritional values = 200 calories | 4g protein | 14g fat | 18g carbohydrates

Chapter 8:

The Anti-Inflammatory Lifestyle

8.1 Stress Management Techniques

Navigating the complexities of modern life, it's imperative to cultivate a sanctuary of calm within ourselves. The art of stress management is not a luxury but a necessity, especially when we consider its inflammatory implications. Adapting tailored techniques to ward off stress can effectively bolster our anti-inflammatory lifestyle and contribute to our overall vitality.

The Essence of Mindfulness: Cultivating Inner Peace

At the core of stress management is the practice of mindfulness – the art of maintaining a moment-by-moment awareness of our thoughts, feelings, bodily sensations, and the surrounding environment. It's about living intentionally, engaging fully with the present, and accepting it without judgment.

- **Meditation:** Establishing a meditation routine is like setting a daily appointment with serenity. Beginning with just a few minutes a day, you can gradually expand this practice to longer periods, fostering tranquility and mental clarity.
- **Mindful Eating:** Approach each meal with intention. Chew slowly, eliminate distractions, and notice how your food impacts your senses and emotions. This simple practice not only enhances digestion but also serves as a form of mindful meditation that can reduce stress.

- **Gratitude Journaling:** This is a reflective practice that orients the mind towards positive elements of daily life, actively engaging your thoughts in a practice that opposes the stress response.

Nurturing Human Connections: The Comfort of Community

Do not underestimate the power of social support. Humans are inherently social creatures, and our relationships with others can be a profound source of comfort and stress relief.

- **Conversations:** Heartfelt discussions can help process feelings, providing a different perspective and a chance to release bottled-up emotions.
- **Support Systems:** Building a network – whether friends, family, or support groups – can provide a safety net when stress becomes burdensome.

Breathing Techniques: The Subtlety of the Breath

Breathing is an autonomic function that we often pay little attention to, yet it's an instantly accessible tool to combat stress.

- **Deep Breathing Exercises:** Deep, diaphragmatic breathing sends a message to the brain to calm down and relax, and the brain then forwards this message to the body.

How to Practice Deep Breathing:

1) **Find a Comfortable Position:**
   Sit in a chair with your feet flat on the floor, or lie on your back with a pillow under your head and knees.
2) **Place Your Hands:**
   Put one hand on your chest and the other on your abdomen to feel the correct movement of your diaphragm.

3) Inhale Slowly:

Breathe in slowly through your nose, expanding your belly while keeping your chest relatively still. Visualize your lungs filling with air from the bottom up.

4) Hold the Breath:

Hold the breath briefly for a count of 2-3 seconds.

5) Exhale Slowly:

Gently breathe out through your mouth or nose (whichever feels more comfortable), allowing your abdomen to fall. It should take longer to exhale than it did to inhale.

6) Repeat:

Continue this pattern for several minutes. Aim for six to ten deep, slow breaths per minute.

- **Rhythmic Breathing:** Developing a routine that incorporates rhythmic breathing can help return the body to a less stressed state in a matter of minutes.

How to Practice Rhythmic Breathing:

1) Maintain a Comfortable Posture:

Like with deep breathing, sit or lie in a comfortable position.

2) Set a Breathing Cycle:

Choose a count for breathing in, holding, and breathing out. A simple pattern is the 4-4-4-4 cycle (in for 4, hold for 4, out for 4, hold for 4). However, you can adjust the numbers according to your lung capacity and comfort level.

3) Focus on Evenness:

With rhythmic breathing, the emphasis is on the consistency of your breaths. Try to make your inhales and exhales the same duration.

4) Engage Your Diaphragm:

Although the focus is not specifically on deep breathing, it's still important to use your diaphragm to fill your lungs efficiently.

5) Find Your Rhythm:

Start the breathing pattern, keeping it smooth and steady. Continue for several minutes until you feel a sense of calm.

6) Experiment with Ratios:

For stress reduction, some people find longer exhales to be more calming. You might experiment with a 4-4-6-2 pattern (4 seconds in, hold for 4, 6 seconds out, hold for 2) or whatever rhythm feels soothing.

Harnessing Creativity and Hobbies: Engagement and Escapism

Immersing in creative activities or hobbies is more than just idle pastime; it's an active stress-reducing practice that can divert the mind from stressors and provide a sense of accomplishment and joy.

- **Artistic Pursuits:** Painting, drawing, or crafting can be meditative and liberating experiences that allow for emotional expression without words.
- **Gardening or Cooking:** These activities promote mindfulness and can be therapeutic, creating something beautiful or delicious from the effort.

Reconnecting with Nature: The Healing Touch of the Earth

Interacting with the natural world offers an escape from the stress of the electronic age. Nature's inherent serenity acts as a soothing balm for the overstimulated mind.

- **Outdoor Activities:** Whether it's a leisurely stroll, sitting by a body of water, or simply breathing in fresh air, nature provides a space for restorative calm and introspection.

Integrating Stress Management into Daily Rituals

Incorporating stress management techniques into daily life need not be onerous. Small, consistent practices can integrate seamlessly into your routine, compounding over time to build resilience against stress.

- **Habit Pairing:** Tying a stress-reducing practice with a daily habit, like taking deep breaths while waiting for your morning coffee, can form the foundation of a sustainable routine.

In essence, managing stress is about nurturing your mind, spirit, and body in various ways that resonate personally. It's about creating a tapestry of techniques that soothes, replenishes, and fortifies. Each stress management practice you adopt is a step toward a more peaceful inner world, complementing your anti-inflammatory lifestyle and contributing to a more vibrant, balanced state of health.

8.2 Importance of Sleep and Relaxation

In the fast-paced cadence of modern life, a restful night's slumber can become an elusive ideal, yet the restorative power of quality sleep and relaxation stands as a cornerstone in the edifice of an anti-inflammatory lifestyle. Those seeking to mitigate inflammation and enhance overall health must recognize sleep not as a luxury, but as a non-negotiable pillar of well-being.

Sleep: The Unsung Hero of Well-being

Robust sleep is vital in allowing the body's tissues to repair, the brain to detoxify, and the immune system to recalibrate. Chronic sleep deprivation, meanwhile, ignites a cascade of hormonal imbalances and triggers inflammatory pathways. The architecture of a healthy sleep routine is intricate, with periods of deep slumber intermingled with lighter stages, each serving specific functions crucial to maintaining physical and cognitive health. This nightly reset underwrites the body's defenses against inflammatory assaults, with research underscoring that adults should strive for approximately 7-9 hours of sleep per night to harness these benefits.

Relaxation: Quieting the Inflammatory Response

In the absence of relaxation, the body's stress response remains activated, like an engine perpetually idling, straining every biological system. Chronic stress—the incessant exposure to cortisol and other stress hormones—fans the flames of inflammation and disrupts immune function. In contrast, relaxation practices such as deep breathing exercises, progressive muscle relaxation, or mindfulness can help cool down this inflammatory response, nurturing the body back to a more balanced state.

Sleep, Diet, and Inflammation: An Intertwined Narrative

The relationship between sleep, relaxation, and an anti-inflammatory diet is a dynamic trilogy that influences the inflammatory process. Poor sleep can alter appetite hormones, leading to cravings and subsequent poor dietary choices that exacerbate existing inflammation. On the flip side, a diet rich in anti-inflammatory foods can pave the road to restorative sleep, fostering a virtuous cycle of wellness. Furthermore, relaxation practices can modulate appetite and improve dietary decisions, highlighting the interconnectedness of these lifestyle elements.

Creating a Sanctuary for Sleep

To foster a conducive environment for sleep, consider your bedroom a sanctuary devoted to rest. The physical milieu should be cool, dark, and quiet, inviting a sense of tranquility and peace. Evaluate your mattress and pillows for comfort and support, as they are the substrates on which quality slumber relies. Also, prioritize making a clear demarcation between the areas for work and rest within the home.

Establishing a Pre-Sleep Ritual

Humans are creatures of habit, and the body thrives on routines that signify the approach of bedtime. It is important to establish a pre-sleep ritual that may include unwinding activities such as reading, gentle stretching, or relaxation techniques. Minimize exposure to the blue light emanating from screens, as it can impede the production of melatonin, the hormone that orchestrates the sleep-wake cycle.

Balancing Act: Sleep Hygiene and Daily Responsibilities

While setting the stage for optimal sleep and relaxation is crucial, many find themselves juggling sleep with other daily demands. Recognizing that the diverse tasks of your day require appropriate energy levels can assist in prioritizing sleep not as an afterthought, but as a foundational element of health. Develop a flexible but consistent sleep schedule that aligns with your natural rhythms and lifestyle, understanding that occasional deviations are inevitable but should not become the norm.

Relaxation Techniques for an Anti-Inflammatory Life

Even brief periods of relaxation can produce anti-inflammatory effects, and practices can be thoughtfully woven into the fabric of your day. Brief meditative pauses, for instance, can serve as restorative islands in a sea of obligations. Alternatively, engaging in hobbies or listening to music can also provide periods of mental and emotional reprieve, attenuating the body's stress response.

Monitoring Progress

As with any lifestyle change, observing the transformative effects of improved sleep and relaxation is instrumental in sustaining motivation. Keeping a record of your sleep duration, quality, relaxation practices, and consequent energy levels can help illuminate the beneficial influences on your inflammatory status and overall vitality.

8.3 Daily Movement and Exercise

The Dynamic Duo: Movement and Exercise in the Anti-Inflammatory Arsenal
When the subject of neutralizing inflammation arises, movement and exercise should be given a marquee spot on your calendar, not penciled in as an afterthought. For those pursuing the anti-inflammatory lifestyle, incorporating regular physical activity is not just about building muscle or shedding pounds; it's about sparking a profound internal shift that quenches the fires of chronic inflammation.

The Biology of Motion

Each time our muscles contract, they send out a battalion of molecules that have far-reaching effects on our inflammatory status. These include myokines, which work similar to emissaries, dispatched with messages that suppress inflammatory markers and fortify the immune system. By engaging in daily movement, we are effectively enlisting our physiology in combatting inflammation at the cellular level.

Exercise: A Prescription for Healthy Aging

Aging and inflammation are close kin, with time often fanning the flames of chronic inflammation. However, exercise can be a potent antidote, protecting our cells from the slow burn of age-related diseases. It's no hyperbole to state that a commitment to movement can mediate the life-long dialogue between our biology and the passage of time.

The Exercise Spectrum

Understanding that the term 'exercise' encompasses a broad array of activities is crucial. Whether it's structured gym routines, swimming laps, or simply walking the dog, the goal is consistent engagement in physical activities that resonate with your lifestyle and preferences. The key is to discover what form of exercise sparks joy for you—this ensures it becomes a sustainable, and integral component of your daily life.

Unshackling from Intensity Myths

Let's dispel a myth: effective exercise does not equate to gut-wrenching, high-intensity workouts. For those intimidated by the prospect of exercise, know that moderate-intensity activities can be just as effective in curbing inflammation. It's about finding balance and leaning into the type of physical engagement that is doable and enjoyable for you.

The Subtle Art of Incorporating Movement

Seamlessly integrating movement into your day may require a gentle shift in perspective. Instead of viewing exercise as a separate entity, blend it into the tapestry of your daily activities: take the stairs instead of the elevator, engage in walking meetings, or perform stretches while watching TV. Look for opportunities to add steps and stretch your limbs—a little creativity goes a long way.

Resistance Training and Inflammation

Resistance exercise isn't simply about gaining strength—it plays a direct role in managing inflammation. Lifting weights, even with light resistance, fosters muscle growth and resilience, which in turn has a systemic effect. Muscles act as a sink for glucose and a source of anti-inflammatory signals, making them valuable allies in your health pursuits.

The Restorative Power of Post-Exercise

The period following exercise is a time of recovery and repair. This is when the body diligently works to heal the micro-damage caused by physical exertion—a process that, whilst it might sound counterintuitive, helps lower long-term inflammation. The body swings into a restorative mode, fortifying itself against future stressors.

Consistency Over Intensity

Consistency in exercise trumps episodic intense workouts. The latter can often lead to injury or burnout, while regular, manageable exercise sessions build a foundation of resilience against chronic inflammation. Aim for regularity in your routine, allowing for rest and mix up different types of activities to engage different muscle groups and avoid monotony.

Exercise as a Conduit to Better Nutrition

Engaging in regular physical activity has a symbiotic relationship with good eating habits. Often, those who maintain an active lifestyle are more inclined to reach for nourishing, anti-inflammatory foods, creating a feedback loop that supports both dietary goals and physical vigor.

Mastering the Art of Self-Paced Exercise

Listening to your body and adjusting your exercise routine accordingly is the hallmark of a sustainable practice. Start where you're comfortable, and gradually build up the intensity and duration as your fitness improves. This is not a race, but rather a thoughtful cultivation of well-being that respects your body's signals.

The Future You: The Long-Term Vision of Daily Movement and Exercise

Envision the future you: a person who has embraced movement as part of their identity. This future self is more resilient, vital, and primed to thrive in an environment of reduced inflammation. Daily movement and exercise aren't just a chapter in a wellness book—they're written into the narrative of your life, propelling you toward a healthier, more vibrant future.

Chapter 9:

The 30-Day Anti-Inflammatory Challenge

9.1 Balanced Macronutrient Ratios

Balanced Macronutrient Ratios

At the heart of the anti-inflammatory diet is an understanding that not all calories are created equal, and the right mix of proteins, fats, and carbohydrates can turn everyday meals into powerful tools for combating inflammation.

The Foundation: Proteins, Fats, and Carbohydrates

The cornerstone of any well-designed anti-inflammatory meal plan is the balanced interaction between proteins, fats, and carbohydrates. This trio of macronutrients plays a pivotal role in regulating the body's inflammatory responses. However, the key is not just in selecting anti-inflammatory foods but in balancing these macronutrients to support your body's healing processes.

Proteins are essential for repairing tissue damage and are fundamental components of an anti-inflammatory diet. Opting for lean proteins, such as fish rich in omega-3 fatty acids, can provide dual benefits: supplying the body with necessary amino acids while further reducing inflammation.

Fats, particularly those found in avocados, nuts, seeds, and olives, are rich in anti-inflammatory omega-3 fatty acids. Incorporating these healthy fats into your diet supports cell health and moderates the body's inflammatory processes. The magic lies not just in consuming fats, but in ensuring a balance between omega-3 and omega-6 fatty acids, tipping the scales in favor of inflammation reduction.

Carbohydrates have often been wrongly vilified. In truth, the focus should be on complex carbohydrates, such as those found in vegetables, fruits, and whole grains. These foods are rich in fiber, which can help to regulate the body's insulin response and provide a steady source of energy, minimizing spikes in blood sugar that can lead to inflammation.

Crafting Your Plate

The question then becomes: How do we apply this knowledge in a practical, accessible way without turning meal preparation into an overwhelming task?

Imagine your plate divided into three sections. One-half of your plate should be filled with colorful, fiber-rich vegetables – these are your carbohydrates. One-quarter should hold a lean protein source, and the remaining quarter should contain healthy fats.

This simple visualization serves as a daily guide for creating balanced, anti-inflammatory meals without the need for complicated calculations or strict measurements. It emphasizes the importance of variety, not just in flavors but in the nutrients that different foods offer, cultivating a balanced ecosystem within your body that can withstand and combat inflammation.

Recognizing the Signals

Understanding how your body responds to different macronutrient ratios is crucial. Some may find they thrive on a slightly higher proportion of healthy fats, while others may need more protein to feel their best. It's important to listen to your body's signals – energy levels, satiety after meals, digestive comfort – and adjust your ratios accordingly.

This responsiveness to the body's feedback is a powerful tool in fine-tuning your diet to more effectively fight inflammation. It acknowledges that while the principles of the anti-inflammatory diet are universal, the application is deeply personal.

The Role of Whole Foods

Integral to balancing macronutrients is the commitment to whole, minimally processed foods. These foods are naturally designed to provide the optimal balance of nutrients our bodies need. By choosing whole foods, we sidestep the pitfalls of added sugars, processed fats, and refined carbohydrates, all of which can contribute to inflammation.

In conclusion, the challenge of the next 30 days is to incorporate balanced macronutrient ratios into each meal, focusing on whole foods and listening to your body's feedback. This approach not only simplifies the concept of the anti-inflammatory diet but also demystifies the process, making it accessible and sustainable for all. It's about making informed, conscious choices that not only satiate the palate but also support your body's natural resilience against inflammation.

9.2 Efficient Meal Prep Tips

Success in adopting an anti-inflammatory diet begins with meticulous planning. Before the rush of the week takes hold, set aside a moment to plan your meals. This includes not just what you'll eat, but when you'll prepare it. Create a schedule that outlines your meals for the week, including snacks. The aim here is to anticipate your dietary needs, thus minimizing the likelihood of resorting to inflammatory convenience foods during busy moments.

Consider batch cooking, a powerful strategy where you prepare several servings of a dish at once. It's efficient, saves time, and ensures you have a ready supply of nutritious meals at hand. For example, cooking a large pot of quinoa at the beginning of the week allows you to use it as a versatile base for different meals, from breakfast porridge to a hearty dinner salad.

Simplify Shopping: Streamline Your Ingredients
When shopping for your anti-inflammatory pantry, focus on simplicity and versatility. Ingredients that can be used in multiple recipes reduce waste and cut down on costs. Prioritize fresh, whole foods like vegetables, fruits, lean proteins, and healthy fats. These

staples form the backbone of the anti-inflammatory diet and can be mixed and matched to create an array of satisfying meals.

Equip yourself with a detailed shopping list organized by food categories. This not only speeds up your shopping trip but also helps you navigate the temptations of processed foods that can derail your dietary goals. Additionally, consider investing in anti-inflammatory herbs and spices, such as turmeric and ginger, which can transform simple dishes into flavorful, health-boosting meals.

Utilize Time-Saving Cooking Techniques

Efficient cooking techniques can drastically reduce time spent in the kitchen while preserving the nutritional integrity of your food. Steaming, for example, is a quick method that retains the vibrant flavors and health benefits of vegetables. Utilizing a slow cooker or pressure cooker for legumes and tough cuts of meat can tenderize these ingredients without constant monitoring.

Where possible, prepare components of your meals in advance. Dicing vegetables, marinating proteins, or prepping salad dressings ahead of time streamlines the cooking process. These ready-to-go ingredients can then be quickly assembled into meals, saving precious time during busy weekdays.

Embrace Leftovers: The Art of Repurposing

Viewing leftovers as a foundation for new meals can inspire creativity and reduce food waste. A grilled chicken breast from dinner, for example, can be repurposed into a savory chicken salad for lunch the next day. Roasted vegetables can be transformed into a vibrant breakfast hash. By changing the context of these ingredients, you maintain meal variety without additional prep work.

Enlist Tools and Technology

In today's world, numerous tools and apps are available to aid in meal planning and preparation. Use technology to your advantage by seeking out meal planning apps that cater to anti-inflammatory diets. Many of these platforms offer customizable meal plans, organized shopping lists, and even delivery options for your ingredients.

9.3 30-Day Meal Plans

Day	Breakfast	Lunch	Dinner	Snack
1	Berry Bliss Smoothie	Crunchy Kale and Chickpea Salad	Lemon and Dill Baked Salmon + Garlic Roasted Brussels Sprouts	Avocado Chocolate Mousse
2	Sunrise Berry Coconut Bowl	Mediterranean Artichoke and Tomato Salad	Herbed Grilled Chicken Breast + Ginger Turmeric Cauliflower Rice	Coconut Almond Energy Balls
3	Turmeric Tofu Scramble	Lentil and Kale Stew	Spicy Black Bean and Quinoa Salad	Baked Apple Cinnamon Chips
4	Chia and Hemp Seed Pudding	Rainbow Quinoa and Veggie Salad	Garlic Shrimp with Zucchini Noodles + Lemon Garlic Steamed Asparagus	Berry Coconut Yogurt Parfait
5	Spiced Sweet Potato Muffins	Sweet Potato and Black Bean Chili	Turmeric Chicken Stir-Fry + Balsamic Glazed Carrots	Dark Chocolate Pumpkin Seed Bark
6	Green Ginger Antioxidant Shake	Spinach and Avocado Salad with Pomegranate	Lemon Pepper Tuna Steak + Spiced Roasted Sweet Potatoes	Avocado Cilantro Lime Dressing with Veggie Sticks
7	Mediterranean Tofu Scramble Bowl	Mediterranean Chickpea Stew	Baked Trout with Almonds + Repeat of a preferred side dish	Ginger Tahini Sauce with Crudité
8	Blueberry Oat Bars	Butternut Squash and Apple Soup	Spicy Grilled Mackerel + Repeat of a preferred side dish	Sweet Red Pepper and Walnut Dip with Whole Grain Toast
9	Almond and Berry Breakfast Salad	Broccoli and Bean Salad with Almond Dressing	Herb Roasted Salmon with Tomatoes + Repeat of a preferred side dish	Coconut Almond Energy Balls
10	Cinnamon Blueberry Wake-Up Shake	Gingery Mushroom and Barley Soup	Sage and Thyme Chicken Breast + Repeat of a preferred side dish	Avocado Chocolate Mousse
11	Green Goodness Bowl	Turmeric Ginger Carrot Soup	Lemon Garlic Roasted Chicken Thighs + Lemon Garlic Steamed Asparagus	Baked Apple Cinnamon Chips

12	Tropical Turmeric Smoothie	Crunchy Kale and Chickpea Salad	Balsamic Glazed Chicken + Garlic Roasted Brussels Sprouts	Berry Coconut Yogurt Parfait
13	Red Beet Power Smoothie	Spinach and Avocado Salad with Pomegranate	Seared Scallops with Spinach + Ginger Turmeric Cauliflower Rice	Dark Chocolate Pumpkin Seed Bark
14	Avocado Egg Boat Bowl	Mediterranean Artichoke and Tomato Salad	Spicy Paprika Chicken Drumsticks + Balsamic Glazed Carrots	Avocado Chocolate Mousse
15	Smoked Salmon Avocado Wrap	Rainbow Quinoa and Veggie Salad	Lemon Pepper Tuna Steak + Repeat of a preferred side dish	Coconut Almond Energy Balls
16	Spinach and Mushroom Egg Muffins	Butternut Squash and Apple Soup	Mediterranean-Style Baked Haddock + Spiced Roasted Sweet Potatoes	Sweet Red Pepper and Walnut Dip with Whole Grain Toast
17	Cinnamon Blueberry Wake-Up Shake	Ginger Sesame Seed Topping with Avocado Salad	Garlic Shrimp with Zucchini Noodles + Lemon Garlic Steamed Asparagus	Ginger Tahini Sauce with Crudité
18	Sunrise Berry Coconut Bowl	Sweet Potato and Black Bean Chili	Asian-Style Grilled Tilapia + Repeat of a preferred side dish	Avocado Chocolate Mousse
19	Berry Bliss Smoothie	Lentil and Kale Stew	Mustard Glazed Chicken Tenders + Garlic Roasted Brussels Sprouts	Coconut Almond Energy Balls
20	Green Ginger Antioxidant Shake	Spinach and Avocado Salad with Pomegranate + Ginger Sesame Seed Topping	Herb Crusted Cod with Roasted Vegetables + Lemon Garlic Steamed Asparagus	Baked Apple Cinnamon Chips
21	Spiced Sweet Potato Muffins	Gingery Mushroom and Barley Soup	Grilled Lemon Herb Pork Chops + Repeat of a preferred side dish	Avocado Cilantro Lime Dressing with Veggie Sticks
22	Chia and Hemp Seed Pudding	Broccoli and Bean Salad with Almond Dressing	Baked Rainbow Trout with Herbs + Ginger Turmeric Cauliflower Rice	Dark Chocolate Pumpkin Seed Bark
23	Almond and Berry Breakfast Salad	Mediterranean Chickpea Stew	Pan-Seared Duck Breast with Blueberry Sauce + Garlic Roasted Brussels Sprouts	Sweet Red Pepper and Walnut Dip with Whole Grain Toast
24	Green Goodness Bowl	Rainbow Quinoa and Veggie Salad	Spicy Shrimp Tacos with Cabbage Slaw + Balsamic Glazed Carrots	Coconut Almond Energy Balls
25	Tropical Turmeric Smoothie	Turmeric Ginger Carrot Soup	Sesame Crusted Tofu with Kale Salad + Lemon Garlic Steamed Asparagus	Berry Coconut Yogurt Parfait
26	Avocado Egg Boat Bowl	Crunchy Kale and Chickpea Salad	Balsamic Glazed Salmon + Repeat of a preferred side dish	Avocado Chocolate Mousse

27	Smoked Salmon Avocado Wrap	Spinach and Avocado Salad with Pomegranate + Ginger Sesame Seed Topping	Chicken and Asparagus Lemon Stir Fry + Repeat of a preferred side dish	Ginger Tahini Sauce with Crudité
28	Berry Bliss Smoothie	Sweet Potato and Black Bean Chili	Ground Turkey and Quinoa Stuffed Peppers + Spiced Roasted Sweet Potatoes	Baked Apple Cinnamon Chips
29	Cinnamon Blueberry Wake-Up Shake	Lentil and Kale Stew	Grilled Mahi Mahi with Mango Salsa + Repeat of a preferred side dish	Coconut Almond Energy Balls
30	Sunrise Berry Coconut Bowl	Ginger Sesame Seed Topping with Avocado Salad	One-Pot Turmeric Coconut Rice with Greens + Lemon Garlic Steamed Asparagus	Dark Chocolate Pumpkin Seed Bark

9.4 Measuring Inflammation Markers

The Essence of Inflammation Markers

In the intricate dance of health and disease, inflammation plays a leading role—sometimes the protector, sometimes the antagonist. Measuring inflammation markers is akin to decoding the body's cryptic messages, illuminating the state of silent battles waged within. As you cross the threshold from day one to day thirty of your anti-inflammatory journey, quantifying these changes becomes more than an exercise in science; it becomes a beacon of progress, a testament to the power of mindful eating and living.

The Bridge Between Diet and Inflammation

Our bodies are not mere bystanders in the world of biochemistry; they are active participants, responding to every nutrient and insult with precision. The anti-inflammatory diet is designed with this responsiveness in mind, aiming to dial down the body's inflammatory response. Foods rich in omega-3 fatty acids, antioxidants, and phytonutrients have taken center stage in your meals, each playing their role in modulating inflammation.

The Markers: A Closer Look

- C-Reactive Protein (CRP): A herald of inflammation. Elevated in cases of acute and chronic inflammation, CRP levels serve as a harbinger of inflammatory states in the body. A decrease in CRP can often correlate with a reduction in inflammation-related symptoms, making it a focal point in post-challenge evaluations.

- Interleukins (IL): These cellular messengers, notably IL-6 and IL-10, are intricately involved in the body's inflammation narrative, each telling a part of the story. IL-6, often vilified for its pro-inflammatory role, contrasts with IL-10's calming, anti-inflammatory effects. The balance between these and other cytokines provides insights into the body's ongoing inflammatory response and its modulation through dietary changes.

- Tumor Necrosis Factor-alpha (TNF-α): Another key player, TNF-α's levels reflect the intensity of the inflammatory response. Integral to inflammation and immune system signaling, a decrease in TNF-α is indicative of reduced inflammation.

Practical Steps for Evaluation

As the 30-day mark approaches, scheduling a follow-up blood test to measure these markers is essential. Comparing these readings with the baseline values obtained at the beginning of the challenge will reveal the physiological impact of your dietary choices.

Measuring Success Beyond the Numbers

While the reduction in these biomarkers can validate the effects of the anti-inflammatory diet, the true measure of success extends beyond the numerics. The alleviation of symptoms—be it through enhanced mobility, improved digestive health, or a general upliftment in mood—parallels the quantitative data, offering a holistic view of the challenge's outcomes.

Empowering Self-Monitoring: Home Evaluation of Inflammation

Indeed, not every aspect of inflammation requires a microscope or a blood test to be evaluated. As you become an active participant in monitoring your health, there exist scales and self-assessment tools enabling you to gauge inflammation's impact from the comfort of your home. These tools serve as a complement to the clinical biomarker assessments and help bridge the gap between professional medical evaluations and personal health awareness.

- **Visual Analog Scales (VAS):** Commonly used in clinical settings to assess pain, Visual Analog Scales can also be an effective tool for self-assessment. By marking a point on a line that represents the continuum of your pain experience or other inflammation-related symptoms, you develop a personalized record of your daily status.

- **Symptom Diaries:** Keeping a detailed journal of your symptoms, diet, and exercise, can reveal patterns and correlations that you might not notice otherwise. Over time, tracking your symptoms can help you understand how your body responds to certain foods, stress, and lifestyle changes, making it easier to identify what works best for you.

- **Digital Health Tracking:** The market is replete with mobile apps designed for health tracking. These digital tools often incorporate symptom checkers, mood logs, and even dietary tracking that can shed light on your inflammation levels. They can help you visualize progress and reveal insights about your health and lifestyle choices.

The beauty of these self-assessment tools lies in their simplicity and their ability to render a sometimes abstract concept into a manageable and trackable aspect of daily life. As you transition from the end of the challenge into a lifelong journey of wellness, these tools can continue to serve as personal health allies, ensuring that the lessons learned become a seamless part of your continuous commitment to an anti-inflammatory lifestyle.

Beyond the 30-Day Challenge

The conclusion of the challenge is not an end but a new beginning. Armed with knowledge and empirical evidence of how dietary interventions can sway the markers of inflammation, the way forward involves nurturing the habits cultivated over the past 30 days. This continued commitment can sustain the gains achieved and further propel you toward optimal health and well-being.

9.5 Monitoring Symptoms and Progress

As you maneuver through this period, the crucial aspect to keep tabs on is your own body. It's about understanding the shifts that occur when you introduce a myriad of nutrient-dense, anti-inflammatory foods into your diet and reducing those that may trigger inflammation. This chapter serves as your compass to navigate these changes, offering you concrete strategies to monitor symptoms and gauge progress effectively.

The essence of monitoring lies in creating a bridge between your current state and your desired health goals. Every individual responds differently to dietary changes; hence, personalizing your approach is key. This process ensures you're not only aware of the positive transformations but also mindful of any adverse reactions your body may exhibit.

Creating Your Health Gauge

First and foremost, establish your baseline. Before diving into the nutritional overhaul, take stock of how you feel. Note your energy levels, sleep quality, digestion, mood, and any specific symptoms of inflammation you experience. Use this baseline as a reference point to assess changes over time.

As days progress into weeks, you'll want to keep a detailed journal. This isn't merely a dietary log but a comprehensive record encompassing various facets of your well-being.

Document what you eat, yes, but also how you feel physically and emotionally. Note any fluctuations in symptoms, sleep patterns, energy levels, and overall mood.

Integrating Subjective and Objective Measures

Pain, stiffness, digestive issues, and fatigue are subjective symptoms, perceived and experienced only by you. Their intensity can be assessed using simple scales, like the Numeric Rating Scale (from 0, no symptom, to 10, worst possible symptom). Regularly scoring your symptoms can help visualize the impact of dietary changes over time.

Then there's the objective side of the equation. Certain parameters, like body weight, blood pressure, and, if possible, inflammatory markers through lab tests, offer quantifiable data. Tracking these metrics provides a tangible way to measure the physical changes your body undergoes as you adapt to an anti-inflammatory lifestyle.

Recognizing Patterns and Adjusting Course

Through diligent monitoring, patterns will emerge. Perhaps certain foods exacerbate your symptoms, or maybe you discover that you function better with a higher intake of specific nutrients. This phase is about connecting the dots between your diet and the way you feel. It's crucial to remain adaptable, making adjustments to your meal plan based on the feedback your body provides.

Measuring Success Beyond Symptoms

Success in the 30-Day Challenge isn't solely measured by the reduction of symptoms. It's also seen in the enhancement of your overall quality of life. Improved energy levels, better sleep quality, and a more stable mood are all hallmarks of success. These broader health improvements underline the efficacy of an anti-inflammatory diet, reinforcing the importance of a holistic approach to health.

As you move forward, remember that health isn't a destination but a dynamic process. The 30-Day Anti-Inflammatory Challenge equips you with the tools to make informed, health-enhancing decisions daily, encouraging a relationship with food that is both nurturing and transformative. Through mindful monitoring and sustained effort, you can achieve the balance and well-being you seek.

Conclusion

As we draw the curtains on our journey together through the realms of anti-inflammatory living, I find myself reflecting on the multitude of steps we've taken side by side. Through the pages of this book, we've embarked on a voyage towards understanding chronic inflammation, unraveling its complexities, and harnessing the power of food to fight back. I penned this book with a singular vision in mind – to illuminate the path for you towards optimal health, using the guiding light of evidence-based nutritional wisdom.

The road to wellness is as much about the steps we take as it is about the mindset with which we embark on this path. It's been my earnest effort to not only provide you with the understanding and tools needed to combat inflammation through diet but also to instill in you a sense of empowered responsibility towards your health. The choices you make at the dining table ripple far beyond the immediate moments of satisfaction they provide, influencing your health, vitality, and quality of life in profound ways.

If there's one cornerstone principle I hope you take away from our time together, it's that the journey towards an anti-inflammatory lifestyle is not marked by scarcity or restriction. Rather, it's a rich exploration of the diversity and abundance nature offers us. The plethora of anti-inflammatory foods detailed throughout this book is testament to the fact that healthful eating can be wonderfully enjoyable, full of flavor, and deeply satisfying.

I've endeavored to make this guidestress-free and accessible, breaking down the science into digestible insights and providing practical, budget-friendly solutions for adopting an anti-inflammatory diet. Remember, every small step counts. Whether it's incorporating more leafy greens into your diet, experimenting with anti-inflammatory spices, or simply choosing water over sugary beverages, each choice is a powerful statement of your commitment to your health.

It's also crucial to understand that while diet plays a starring role in managing inflammation, it's but one piece of the wellness puzzle. Stress management, quality sleep, regular physical activity, and nurturing positive mental health are equally important. I encourage you to harness the principles outlined in this book not as a rigid regimen but as flexible guidelines to weave into the fabric of your life, creating a holistic approach to wellness that is sustainable, enjoyable, and deeply nourishing.

As you move forward from here, armed with the knowledge and tools to sculpt a healthier, more vibrant version of yourself, remember that this is a journey of discovery. You are bound to encounter challenges and setbacks along the way. Embrace these not as failures but as opportunities for growth and learning. Listen to your body, be patient with yourself, and celebrate every victory, no matter how small.

In closing, I want to extend my heartfelt gratitude to you for allowing me the honor of being a part of your health journey. It is my deepest hope that this book serves not just as a guide but as a companion on your path to wellness. The journey doesn't end here – it's an ongoing adventure, rich with opportunities for personal growth and transformation.

May the lessons learned and practices adopted during the 30-Day Anti-Inflammatory Challenge inspire you to continue exploring, experimenting, and embracing a lifestyle that supports your health and happiness. Here's to a lifetime of vitality, joy, and abundant well-being.

With warmth and wellness,

Dr. Madison Wells

Made in the USA
Las Vegas, NV
05 June 2024

90751446R00059